Designed for Digital

Management on the Cutting Edge Series from MIT Sloan Management Review

Edited by Paul Michelman

Published in cooperation with *MIT Sloan Management Review*

The AI Advantage: How to Put the Artificial Intelligence Revolution to Work
Thomas H. Davenport

The Technology Fallacy: How People Are the Real Key to Digital Transformation
Gerald C. Kane, Anh Nguyen Phillips, Jonathan Copulsky, and Garth Andrus

Designed for Digital: How to Architect Your Business for Sustained Success
Jeanne W. Ross, Cynthia M. Beath, and Martin Mocker

Designed for Digital

How to Architect Your Business for Sustained Success

Jeanne W. Ross, Cynthia M. Beath,
and Martin Mocker

The MIT Press
Cambridge, Massachusetts
London, England

This book was set in Stone Serif and Stone Sans by Westchester Publishing Services. Printed and bound in the United States of America.

Library of Congress Cataloging-in-Publication Data

Names: Ross, Jeanne W., author. | Beath, Cynthia Mathis, author. | Mocker, Martin, author.
Title: Designed for digital : how to architect your business for sustained success / Jeanne W. Ross, Cynthia M. Beath, and Martin Mocker.
Description: Cambridge, MA : MIT Press, [2019] | Series: Management on the cutting edge | Includes bibliographical references and index.
Identifiers: LCCN 2018059707 | ISBN 9780262042888 (hardcover : alk. paper)
Subjects: LCSH: Information technology--Management. | Entrepreneurship--Technological innovations.
Classification: LCC HD30.2 .R6637 2019 | DDC 658--dc23 LC record available at https://lccn.loc.gov/2018059707

10 9 8 7 6 5 4 3

Contents

Series Foreword

The world does not lack for management ideas. Thousands of researchers, practitioners, and other experts produce tens of thousands of articles, books, papers, posts, and podcasts each year. But only a scant few promise to truly move the needle on practice, and fewer still dare to reach into the future of what management will become. It is this rare breed of idea—meaningful to practice, grounded in evidence, and *built for the future*—that we seek to present in this series.

Paul Michelman
Editor in chief
MIT Sloan Management Review

Preface and Acknowledgments

As consumers, we take digital technologies for granted. No longer are we impressed that anytime, anywhere, we can shop, hire a ride, reserve a table at a restaurant, pay our bills, view a favorite movie, find a new recipe, or learn popular remedies for our latest ailment. We don't wonder why these things are possible; we simply expect them.

If you're working in a "big, old" company, you know that the adoption of digital technologies in business doesn't come as naturally. Inserting digital technologies to enhance operations and create new value propositions has proven extremely challenging. This raises the question: If digital technologies are consistently making our consumer lives easier, why aren't they making it easier to succeed in business? Why are business leaders anxious about digital disruption rather than marveling about how quickly they can provide new, exciting, and ever-improving digital solutions to their customers?

Five years of research have led us to believe that the answer to these questions is this: *Big, old companies are simply not designed for digital.*

Business leaders have long taken responsibility for defining strategy, establishing structures, and measuring outcomes to make their companies successful. They are less likely to own responsibility for designing the interactions among their people, processes, and technology to ensure their companies can execute new digital strategies. We argue that business leaders cannot just hope that all the activities in their companies will coalesce in ways that will enable them to figure out how to solve customer problems and rapidly deliver new, digitally inspired value propositions. They must design their companies for digital success.

That is why we wrote this book. In our research at big companies, we found that, although digital is all about speed, a digital transformation is a long journey. That's because it requires you to (re)design how your company works. While no company has completed the entire journey, a small number of companies are leading the way. By sharing their combined stories and analyzing their experiences, we hope to provide some direction for your journey.

Digital technologies are game changing. Leaders of big, old companies cannot rely on old rules to play this new game. The talents, skills, processes, systems, and roles that made your company successful in the past are quickly becoming irrelevant. If your big old company is going to compete in the digital economy, you must redesign for digital. Nobody says it's easy. But now is the time to get started.

The Research

We were driven to this research by our fascination with enterprise architecture—how companies are designed to execute their strategies. Although most IT leaders have embraced enterprise architecture as a way of mapping a company's IT investments and business process changes, other leaders have been less interested in the topic. We expected that the dawn of digital businesses would lead to widespread embrace of enterprise architecture as a critical senior management tool. We set out to study that phenomenon.

To be honest, that's not what has happened. At least, that's not what happened at most companies. We started the research in 2014 with interviews at 40 large companies about how they were approaching business architecture. Invariably, we were directed to business architects in the IT unit, not a member of the top management team. The most telling finding from that first phase of the research was how hopeful the architects were—and how common it was for them to feel their efforts were not having a significant impact on their companies.

We followed up that set of interviews with mini case studies conducted at 27 companies in 2015 and 2016. Working with the Boston

Consulting Group (BCG), we conducted three interviews at each of these companies—usually with a senior business executive, a senior IT executive, and a third person who was engaged in implementing digital strategy. Most of the companies involved in this phase of the study were starting to articulate digital strategies and taking some initial steps to implement them. In the summer of 2016, we conducted a survey of 171 business leaders to better understand the state of the art.

In 2017 and 2018, we took an in-depth look at companies that were making progress on their digital journeys. We developed case studies describing some of these companies' journeys, including Royal Philips, LEGO, Schneider Electric, AUDI AG, Principal Financial Group, and Northwestern Mutual. We supplemented those written cases with additional interviews at the case study sites and a number of other companies, including CarMax, Toyota, DBS Bank, and USAA. In the summer of 2018, we conducted a survey of 150 senior executives at big old companies to again, better understand the state of the art relative to what we'd seen at our research sites and to gauge how much things had changed since 2016.

Our in-depth case studies and survey reports are available as working papers from the MIT Sloan Center for Information Systems Research (CISR). This book represents a synthesis of all the research over the last five years.

To prepare you for what's to come, we want to note that many companies are going through two transformations: one that *digitizes* the company (i.e., uses digital technologies to enhance operational efficiencies) and one that pursues new *digital* value propositions (i.e., uses digital technology to rapidly innovate new digital offerings—the focus of this book). This dual transformation appears to be a requirement to compete in the digital economy. It also makes the challenge of organizational redesign that much harder.

To help you apply what we've learned about digital transformations, this book shares both our key findings and our in-depth stories. We hope you find them useful.

Who Should Read This Book?

This book is written for executives in established (what we call "big, old"—or we could say "successful") companies who want to disrupt rather than be disrupted by digital offerings, and who are seeking a better understanding of how to do exactly that.

We describe the building blocks for a company's digital transformation: from creating a vision for new digitally inspired value propositions, to generating insight about what digital offerings customers are willing to pay for, to delivering the technology and process platforms that power digital offerings, to designing an accountability framework that enables employees to achieve all of this.

While this book is about digital, it is not a technology book. So if you are a manager in marketing, sales, finance, strategy, operations, or HR, this book is for you. You will not be able to delegate digital transformation to your IT colleagues!

If you are an IT architect or other IT leader, we encourage you to read this book and use it to spread the concept of business design inside your company (we think this book makes an excellent gift for your non-IT colleagues!).

For simplicity, we have adopted the word *company* in this book. However, our comments apply equally to all types of organizations—whether they are for profit, not for profit, or public sector.

Digital technologies are disrupting all industries. The companies we studied in the research for this book come from very different industries. And we aim to inspire and enable executives operating in any industry to design their business for digital.

Whom We Would Like to Thank

Our research would simply not be possible without the support of MIT CISR's patron and sponsor firms. We gratefully acknowledge the support, ideas, and camaraderie you have provided not just for this book, but also for 44 years of MIT CISR research.

During the five years of research for this book, we had the privilege to learn from truly inspirational leaders who shared their stories in our case studies. These leaders include: Bernard Gavgani (BNP Paribas); Lucille Mayer (BNY Mellon); Shamim Mohammad (CarMax); Dave Gledhill, Bidyut Dumra, Paul Cobban (DBS Bank); Pablo Ciano (DHL); Federico Flórez (Ferrovial); Mihir Shah (Fidelity); Enrique Avila (ING Direct Spain); Henrik Amsinck and Anders Lerbech Vinther (LEGO Group); Karl Gouverneur (Northwestern Mutual); Edgar van Zoelen, Jeroen Tas, and Frans van Houten (Philips); Gary Scholten, Juan Manuel Vega, and Pedro Atria (Principal Financial); Michael Nilles (Schindler); Hervé Coureil, Alfons Marquez, and Cyril Perducat (Schneider Electric); Anders Ivarsson (Spotify); Zack Hicks (Toyota Motor North America).

Other business executives who have inspired and challenged our thinking include Tom Bayer (CSBS), Shawn Broadfield (Allstate Insurance Company), Rickey Burks, Leonides De O'Campo (McKinsey), Matt Haigh (Westpac), Brad Fedosoff (CIBC), Luis Hernandez (CEMEX), Craig Hopkins (City of San Antonio), Ken Johnsen (Caterpillar), John Kreul (Bemis), Suresh Kumar, Sue Jean Lin (Alcon), Danial Llano (ING-DiBa), Erwin Logt (FrieslandCampina), Meg McCarthy (Aetna), Mark Meyer (TetraPak), Kal Ruberg (Teck Resources), Rob Samuel (Aetna), David Saul (State Street), Greg Schwartz, Joe Spagnoletti, Mattias Ulbrich (Porsche), Christian Umbach (XapiX.io), and Werner Zippold.

We'd like to thank members of BCG's Technology Advantage Practice, who worked with us in securing and developing a number of our early case studies and then debated the findings from those cases. Stuart Scantlebury, Massimo Russo, and Benjamin Rehberg were instrumental in that work.

We also want to thank the hundreds of managers who participated in case study interviews, took the time to answer our many survey questions, and challenged our thinking in interviews, presentations, and executive education sessions.

We are fortunate to have outstanding colleagues at MIT CISR. Nils Fonstad and Kate Moloney participated in much of the research and worked on case studies important to this research. Ina Sebastian joined the team early and has been instrumental in collecting and analyzing data and in writing up research findings. This book would not be possible without her efforts. Lipsa Jha, while a master's student at MIT Sloan, contributed statistical analysis. We've also benefited a great deal from research discussions with MIT CISR colleagues, Kristine Dery, Wanda Orlikowski, Joe Peppard, Nick van der Meulen, Peter Weill, Barb Wixom, and Stephanie Woerner. MIT CISR colleague Cheryl Miller edited every single case study—and made each of them better.

We'd like to thank MIT CISR visiting scholars, who have stimulated our thinking, introduced us to interesting companies, and challenged our ideas: Peter Andersen (Aarhus University), Abayomi Baiyere (Copenhagen Business School), Daniel Beimborn (Frankfort School of Finance and Management), Siew Kien Sia (Nanyang Technological University), Monideepa Tarafdar (Lancaster University), and Eric van Heck (Rotterdam School of Management).

In addition, we have benefited from the research and feedback of John Mooney at Pepperdine University, Ulrike Schultze at Southern Methodist University, and Christina Soh and Soon Ang at Nanyang Technological University

We are indebted to the individuals who have read and provided feedback on the manuscript at various stages of completion. Thank you to our three anonymous reviewers and to Peter Coffee at Salesforce, as well as MIT CISR colleagues S. K. Sia, Daniel Beimborn, Leslie Owens, Joe Peppard, and Peter Weill. We hope you see evidence of your feedback in the final work. And a special thank you to Emily Taber, our editor at MIT Press, who appeared to thoughtfully consider every single sentence we wrote. You forced us to understand and articulate things we'd taken for granted—or didn't realize we knew.

A huge thank you to MIT CISR's associate director, Chris Foglia, for your patience, creativity, and dedication. Chris has been on a journey with us as we've gradually envisioned research findings in figures and graphics. It was Chris who brought all the pieces together to deliver the final manuscript.

We appreciate all that Amber Franey and Aman Shah do as they work behind the scenes at MIT CISR to keep the train on the tracks. It is a joy to work with you. And thanks to Paul Michelman at MIT Sloan Management Review for believing in us and encouraging MIT Press to publish this book.

A Personal Note from Jeanne

I first want to thank three people who have been extraordinary blessings in my research career. Jack Rockart brought me to MIT CISR 25 years ago and taught me how to communicate research findings to a practitioner audience. I miss him dearly. Peter Weill reimagined MIT CISR in 2000 and opened a world of research opportunities that I never could have imagined. He has also been a constant source of support, feedback, and enthusiasm. I am immeasurably better at what I do because of Peter. Finally, Leslie Owens came to MIT CISR as Executive Director in 2015 and immediately nourished my passion for doing research. She has given me the gift of time, and wrapped it in encouragement, good humor, and great insights.

My greatest blessing is my husband, Dan. Thank you for your patience and understanding, for taking care of the home front and planning occasional vacations, for reading every word in versions of this book that were too early to be interesting (and thanks for pretending that they were!). Thank you for encouraging me to be the best I can be. Our 41 years have been a fabulous journey. Thanks, too, to my three amazing children, Adam, Julie, and Steffie, and the wonderful people they've added to our family, Kaitlin, Kyle, Ollie, and Sam. You are a constant reminder that there's so much more to life than writing a book!

And thanks to two wonderful friends, researchers, and coauthors. I have thoroughly enjoyed our marvelous adventure.

A Personal Note from Cynthia (aka "Boo")

Many thanks! First and foremost, I would like to thank my husband, Denny McCoy. Thank you, Denny, for not trying to fix my creative challenges for me and for just empathizing with me. Thank you for helping me to be less afraid of the blank page and also more willing to say, "It's done." Thank you for helping me appreciate how important it is to see both forests and trees. Thank you for demonstrating to me what it means to be disciplined while being creative. And I should thank you for persuading me to buy a smartphone and to try social media. I also must thank Dolly Mama for listening uncritically as I babble on our walks, and I sincerely thank my coauthors—to whom I will be indebted forever—for including me on this glorious journey. Finally, many thanks to the universe for giving me everything in life I could ever want.

A Personal Note from Martin

A terrific journey started for me in February 2017 when Jeanne asked whether I'd like to join her and Boo in writing this book. More than 2,000 emails, over 50 video conference calls, 2 unforeseen case studies including trips to Amsterdam and Santiago de Chile, a survey, and uncounted magic moments later, I am sitting at the kitchen table writing these lines. What a ride!

I dedicate this book to my wonderful wife Yvonne—I'd have to write another book for all the things I want to thank you for; you mean the world to me!—and to my parents Ursula and Uwe—thank you for teaching me how to learn and for always being there for your children.

I'd also like to thank a number of other special people: The entire MIT CISR team: Aman, Amber, Barb, Cheryl, Chris, Dorothea, Ina, Jeanne, Joe, Kristine, Leslie, Nick, Nils, Peter, and Stephanie. You've created a truly unique place—thanks for letting me be part of this family for over seven years now. Also, my colleagues at Reutlingen University's ESB Business School, especially the International Business study program team that keeps attracting students who make it so much fun to teach about digital; Ainara Novales and Jana Röcker for accepting all the delayed and postponed meetings because "Martin is working on the book." Edgar van Zoelen of Royal Philips and Werner Zippold, formerly of ING Direct Spain: I owe you a lot for introducing me to truly fascinating transformation stories.

Finally, my coauthors, Jeanne and Boo: I wish everyone could have the experience I had. And I hope our readers get as much learning and fun out of reading the book as I had when working on it with you.

1 Digital Business Design

Welcome to the digital economy! If you're reading this book, you are well aware that companies are being bombarded with digital technologies: social, mobile, analytics, cloud, the Internet of Things, all represented aptly by the acronym SMACIT (pronounced *smack it* to reflect how we experience this attack). SMACIT is just the beginning. Biometrics, robotics, artificial intelligence, blockchain, 3D printing, edge computing, and a steady procession of future technologies all have the potential to disrupt your business.

Digital technologies are game changing because they deliver three capabilities: ubiquitous data, unlimited connectivity, and massive processing power. These three capabilities are changing how we live and how we do business. In our personal lives, they mean we no longer sit around the dinner table and postulate how much rain falls each year in Seattle. We pull out our phones and check.

In business, ubiquitous data means we don't guess what customers want, or who they are, or whether they are loyal. We collect data and learn the answer. Unlimited connectivity means immediate access to anything digital, eliminating bottlenecks and delays. We expect to respond immediately, even proactively, to customer problems. Finally, unlimited processing power means we can expect (and afford) systems to crunch all that ubiquitous data to detect relationships humans cannot observe.

To grasp the impact of the capabilities of digital technologies, consider how Uber disrupted an industry. Uber didn't change customer demand for the core product—hired rides. Uber reimagined the value proposition associated with hired rides. In addition to a ride, people could know when the ride would arrive, how much it would cost, and when they would arrive at their destination. Plus, paying for (and providing feedback about) a ride became hassle-free. Taxi companies could have offered such a digital technology–inspired customer solution. They could have preempted Uber or even quickly matched Uber's offerings (yes, even in their more regulated environment). They didn't.

Digital technologies make it possible—and customer demands make it necessary—to solve customer problems rather than just sell a portfolio of products and services. No matter how beloved or essential their existing products, businesses must constantly enhance their customer value propositions[1] to capitalize on the capabilities of digital technologies.

Some not-born-digital companies have already articulated bold visions for new value propositions inspired by the capabilities of digital technologies. For example, Schneider Electric, which traditionally sold electrical equipment, now offers intelligent energy management solutions. USAA wants not only to provide financial services to its globally dispersed members; it wants to deliver integrated solutions that ensure their financial security. Toyota still sells motor vehicles, but it also provides mobility solutions. In addition to selling pet food, Mars, Inc. wants to leverage data to make a better world for pets. These companies are disrupting their businesses in order to solve customer problems.

Digital Offerings Deliver New Value Propositions

This book is devoted to explaining how you can apply digital technologies to fundamentally change your customer value proposition. It's worth noting that digital technologies can also have two important impacts on companies' *existing* products and services.

First, the technologies themselves can enhance the customer experience. Customers want digital channels. The best digital customer experiences include intuitive, convenient apps and other digital interfaces. Digital companies also seamlessly integrate digital and non-digital interactions to enhance customer service.

Second, digital technologies make possible new and improved product features. For example, AI can add autonomous driving features to an automobile manufacturer's core product; the Internet of Things (IoT) and analytics can improve an equipment manufacturer's maintenance services; mobility technologies can allow people to turn on a light, start their car, or unlock a door remotely with a smartphone.

Both of these impacts on existing products and services—better customer experiences and new features—can lead to increased revenues and greater customer satisfaction. We urge you to seize the opportunities they create. But understand that these applications of digital technologies will not disrupt industries. They will raise the bar with regard to customer expectations, but they represent product and service improvements. They do not change your value proposition.

As we noted above, what makes digital technologies disruptive is the opportunity they present for new customer value propositions. These new value propositions stimulate development of *digital offerings*—information-enriched solutions wrapped in a seamless, personalized customer experience. Digital offerings rely on software and data to create new revenue-generating value propositions. Thus, Uber offered not just a ride, but also a solution to the uncertainties, inconveniences, and anxieties associated with navigating a busy city. In fact, Uber prompted some city-dwellers to abandon automobile ownership completely.

Digital offerings are not just for start-ups. USAA, a financial services company for members of the US military, frames the financial needs of its customers (referred to as members) in terms of their life events (buying a car, getting married, buying a house, having kids, planning retirement, being deployed). USAA applies mobile and other digital technologies to create integrated offerings that reduce the hassles and uncertainties associated with each life event. The company's Auto-Circle integrated offering, for example, leverages USAA's and partners' products and services (auto insurance, auto loans, a buying service that secures low prices on new cars) to guide members through a one-stop, online, or mobile app-based car-buying experience—a delightful solution to what can be a stressful life event.[2]

The German car manufacturer AUDI AG is developing offerings that help customers drive an Audi car without actually owning one. For example, "Audi on demand" allows a customer to rent an Audi for a daily fee using a mobile app. For the "Audi at home" digital offering, AUDI collaborates with select luxury residences to offer a shared pool of Audi cars, conveniently parked in the properties' garages. Residents use a mobile app to reserve those cars for personal use. Finally, "Audi shared fleet" provides companies with a virtual car fleet for their employees, who can book a car via a mobile app that charges the employer on a pay-per-use basis.[3]

The purpose of digital offerings like these is to foster revenue growth through new value propositions. Digital technologies can increase customer satisfaction and improve operational excellence, but companies are only dabbling with the opportunities of digital until they start to identify new value propositions.

Reimagining a company's value proposition for the digital economy is not easy. But the bigger conundrum will be piecing together the culture, insights, and competencies that convert a successful pre-digital company into an agile, innovative digital player, capable of using software and data to deliver digital offerings.

Here is the troubling question every leadership team must ask:

Are we capable of delivering a constantly evolving, innovative set of digital offerings?

Our research over four years at nearly 200 companies suggests that for most big companies the answer to this question is no. They cannot deliver digital offerings because they are not designed for digital. That is, the interactions among their people, processes, and technology limit their ability to experiment with, learn from, discard, enhance, reconfigure, and scale up new offerings to provide new value propositions.

Our field research suggests that, in the near-term, digital offerings will represent only a small percentage of most established companies' total revenues. That's because the introduction of digital offerings does not immediately reduce demand for existing products and services. (Still reading paper newspapers and books? Still paying with cash or credit cards?) Companies are developing digital offerings *in addition to,* not instead of, traditional products and services.

Successful companies cannot afford to dump the value propositions that have made them successful—at least not yet. But they also can't afford complacency. You need to start developing digital offerings today, not because they will elevate next quarter's financial results (that's unlikely), but because if you don't start learning how digital technologies can fundamentally change the value of your current products and services, someone else will. Now is the time to start identifying and introducing value propositions driven by ubiquitous data, unlimited connectivity, and massive processing power. In other words, now is the time to design for digital.

Digital Business Design: What It Is and Why You Need It

We define *digital business design* as the holistic organizational configuration of people (roles, accountabilities, structures, skills), processes (workflows, routines, procedures), and technology (infrastructure, applications) to define value propositions and deliver offerings made possible by the capabilities of digital technologies.

Business design is sometimes referred to as business architecture. We are reluctant to use that term because, at many companies, architecture is seen as the IT unit's responsibility. Right now, if you have a business architecture function, it's probably buried in your IT organization (and having limited impact). Digital business design, in contrast, is a responsibility of senior executives in a company. It is how leaders ensure the company can execute its business strategy in a digital economy.

Business design—configuring people, processes and technology for strategy execution—isn't new. Ever since technology became an enabler of business strategy, leaders have wrestled with the need to create synergies among these three organizational design elements. Many companies redesigned their businesses in the 1990s, as they implemented enterprise systems like enterprise resource planning (ERPs, e.g., by the German multinational software corporation SAP) and customer relationship management (CRMs, e.g., by Salesforce) to cut costs and improve the reliability and predictability of core operations. Business leaders learned that successful enterprise system implementations involved more than just new technology. They had to simultaneously introduce streamlined and standardized business processes and new roles, like process and data owners, to accomplish their objectives. The combination of new systems, disciplined processes, transparent data, and new accountabilities enabled companies like Aetna, Campbell Soup, CEMEX, DHL Express, LEGO, and USAA to reduce costs and increase the reliability of their core operations.[4]

Of course, business history offers up many examples of enterprise system implementations that delivered little value. Companies that failed to redesign their business processes or people's roles as they replaced their legacy systems did not realize the desired benefits of enterprise systems.[5] Companies that did not assign ownership of data to business leaders do not have reliable master and transaction data on which to perform analytics or make decisions. Companies without empowered process owners cannot seamlessly integrate acquisitions or enforce standards for new products or regions. Companies that chose to customize their ERPs to fit existing processes, rather than reengineer business processes to leverage new technology capabilities, continue to struggle with operational inefficiencies and customer dissatisfaction today.[6] These companies are paying a price for not designing their business to execute their strategies.

If you struggled to design your company to effectively deploy integrated enterprise systems, brace yourself for digital value propositions. To thrill customers with innovative digital offerings, you need to go way beyond reengineering business processes; you need to rethink how you define, develop, and commercialize customer-facing offerings. You need seamless interactions between your people and automated systems so that customers experience no pain as they move from sales to service and from automated channels to human interactions. To enable that kind of seamlessness, people, processes, and technology must be designed to synchronize decisions and actions across the company.

Synchronization will not happen by accident. You'll need to deliberately configure all three organizational design elements—*people, processes, and technology*—so they deliver on your new value proposition. That is the goal of digital business design.

Amazon Is Designed for Digital

One of the best examples of a company that is designed for digital is Amazon.[7] It's easy to forget that Amazon was born as an online book retailer in 1994. Like most established companies, Amazon had to reimagine its value proposition as new technologies made possible new ways of doing business. Today, Amazon is no longer a book retailer; it's a provider of personal convenience.

Unlike most established companies, Amazon appears to absorb digital capabilities effortlessly as they become viable. For example, when browser adoption spread like wildfire, Amazon shifted from processing orders via semi-automated email exchanges, to letting customers put books in a shopping cart on a website. As adoption of mobile devices took off, Amazon seized the opportunity to create seamless transactions across mobile and web channels. As robot technology matured, Amazon redesigned its fulfillment processes using robots to find and bring items to workers filling orders. Amazon Prime capitalized on those fulfillment processes, offering a new customer value proposition and increasing company revenues.

From the start, Amazon collected detailed data on customer interactions. Amazon extended the value of that data with analytics. By identifying for customers what other customers like them tended to buy, Amazon moved beyond just selling products to helping people find what meets their needs. As machine learning became a viable technology, Amazon exploited its accumulated data to develop more sophisticated insights for the company and more value for its customers.

What is extraordinary about Amazon's success is not simply that it has been inspired by the capabilities of digital technologies to evolve a new value proposition. The more remarkable achievement is that Amazon has almost flawlessly executed its strategy by designing its business to deliver on that evolving value proposition.

Many business and technology leaders will want to attribute Amazon's digital success to its relatively less complex systems environment.

Understandable. Unlike older successful companies, Amazon has not been building messy legacy systems for the last 50 years. But after 20-plus years of systems development, even Amazon has legacy. Its systems include workarounds and inelegant solutions. Nonetheless, there is no question that Amazon's systems are designed for digital. The company's CEO insisted on it. But that is only part of the story.

Consider what has made Amazon's success possible: a well-tuned *process* for testing and learning customer's reactions to new offerings, which relies on *technology* that delivers detailed, reliable data about customers and their desires; and *people* who are fully empowered to design and launch new products, services and concepts. Deft configuration—and constant redesign—of these elements has allowed Amazon to respond rapidly to new customer demands and new technology capabilities. In the process, the company has quickly recovered from (rather than avoided) failed experiments.[8]

Amazon provides a unique example of a company that designs the interactions of people, processes, and technology in pursuit of a digitally inspired business vision. We contend that every company aspiring to be successful in the future needs to be as deliberate in the design of its business.

The daunting challenge for companies trying to design for digital is twofold. First, the extent to which people, process, and technology interact means that any change in design triggers multiple other changes. Second, the breathtaking speed at which new technologies create opportunities for new digital offerings means that those interrelated changes occur almost constantly! Thus, digital design must be fluid. That is why it's worth learning the art of digital design.

Digital Business Design: What It's Not

You might think that CEOs, CIOs, and other C-suite leaders have always assumed responsibility for business design. Think again. Rather than design their companies, most business leaders structure them. They create high-level structures that relegate to lower organizational levels the responsibility for figuring out how to get things done. In other words, they divide and conquer. In doing so, they not only divide responsibility for getting work done; they divide responsibility for much of the people design (e.g., roles, skills), as well as most process and technology design. As a result, there is no organization-wide design; only organization-wide structures.

The advantage of this reliance on structure is that structures help focus the efforts of each organizational unit on delivering a manageable set of specific outcomes (e.g., profitability of a line of business). The disadvantage is that structuring invariably creates organizational silos that impede integration. Siloed organizations are characterized by their efficiencies within silos, not their effectiveness across silos. Recognizing the limitations of silos, leaders invariably introduce matrix structures to provide a single face to their customers and generate enterprise-wide consistency. Matrices can facilitate execution of standard processes for a small set of shared services. They do not however, support development of a constantly evolving set of information-enriched digital offerings.

The problem is that—given their seamlessness—digital offerings require a fast cycle of decisions and actions across functional and business line silos. As siloed companies attempt to deliver digital customer offerings, a growing number of decisions are referred up the hierarchy, discussed across silos, decided by managers far away from the operational reality, and then communicated back to where action will be taken. Digital companies cannot wait for such elongated decision-making processes. And they absolutely cannot afford the lack of synchronization in the decisions and actions of different parts of the business when they are trying to imagine, develop, market, and support digital offerings.

To better understand how to design a company to escape the constraints of business silos, it's useful to understand what digital business design is *not*:

- Digital business design is not restructuring.
- Digital business design is not an end state.
- Digital business design is not IT architecture.

Digital Business Design Is Not Restructuring

At many companies, an announcement of a new business strategy prompts a restructuring. The new structure reflects the company's new priorities—and alignment of power. Leaders announce a restructuring with a fair amount of fanfare, while everyone else awaits such announcements with a fair amount of trepidation.

In digital business design, structure is just one piece of the puzzle that allows leaders to align people with strategic priorities. New roles and accountabilities increasingly supersede structure as the primary mechanisms for defining who does what and in signaling where power is located. This shift from structure to roles is a natural response to a greater need for organizational flexibility. Structure stabilizes; it cordons off resources to a particular business objective. Roles allocate individual attention to emerging—often unclear—business needs.

The new design mimics the design of digital start-ups where teams might own total responsibility for developing, marketing, enhancing, and operating key elements of a company's digital offerings, relying on collaborative technologies and processes to coordinate their activities. In these digital businesses, all three of the design elements—people, processes and technology—are configured to consistently deliver a digital value proposition.

Digital Business Design Is Not an End State

When an architect designs a new building, the blueprints describe the completed building. And when an existing building is undergoing a total renovation, it is vacated. In contrast, when business leaders architect their company, they are designing an entity that is currently in use and constantly changing. There is no end state.

As technologies, customer demands, and strategic opportunities change, a business must adapt. The art of digital business design involves distinguishing what is relatively stable (e.g., core competencies, disciplined enterprise processes, master data structures) from those elements of the business that are expected to change regularly (e.g., digital offerings and features, team goals, apps, and people's roles and skills). Leaders of digital businesses invest in building and maintaining the stable elements while equipping decision makers throughout the company with the data they need to make rapid decisions on anything that must necessarily change. Rather than define an end state, digital business design defines a direction and sets up a company to adapt as the future unfolds.

Digital Business Design Is Not IT Architecture

As we've already noted, most companies locate architecture responsibilities in their IT units. IT architecture matters. It provides a logic that guides the adoption of technology and the development of new systems and enhancements to existing systems. A well-designed IT architecture reduces technology and business risks. IT units can and should take responsibility for IT architecture design.

But the design of a digital business considers far more than technology and systems. It takes a high-level view of the interactions among people, process, and technology. The IT unit is not positioned to design people and processes. Great IT leaders can help shape a vision for digital business design, but the design of a synchronized business requires much broader management engagement.

Of course, executive teams' plates are already full. How can they possibly add digital business design to their responsibilities? We recognize the challenge. It is why we wrote this book. Designing big, old companies for digital success involves devolving accountabilities and embracing reuse. These will not be natural management tendencies for leaders who have learned how to succeed in traditional bureaucracies. Some companies will succeed; some will fail. Our goal is to provide some guidance for your transformation that improves your odds for success.

Digital Business Transformation Is a Long Journey

Many executives in established companies feel an urgency to transform their companies to become digital. This is almost surely because technologies are enabling new value propositions that could eventually render any company's existing value proposition irrelevant. Companies' digital business designs must make them responsive to new possibilities and new customer demands. Realistically, however, it will take time for people—with their processes and technology—to learn how to function as a digital business. Our research has found that transformations in big companies cannot be speedy.

Digital transformations are slow because entrenched habits (i.e., culture) are hard to change. Our research suggests that leaders can best address cultural issues by adopting a series of important new behaviors, as they are needed. Rather than trying to overhaul culture, executives can gradually change specific habits. Introducing new technology and processes provides an opportunity to redesign roles and change habits—and thus eventually culture—one day at a time.

This pace of change is actually a blessing. For the foreseeable future, most companies will continue to generate the bulk of their revenues from their existing value propositions because customers usually expect existing products and services to remain available. So companies can focus first on redesigning just the part of the business that delivers new digital offerings. They can absorb those design changes more broadly as more of the company becomes digital. Thus, they can learn as they go. Royal Philips provides an example of a company navigating a transformation and learning how to succeed as a digital business.

Royal Philips: Transforming to Improve Patient Lives

Royal Philips, a company long known for innovation, has a mission to improve lives with meaningful innovation in healthcare technology.[9] Philips has divested product lines that do not support this approach (e.g., audio/video, lighting) and expanded offerings related to the company's established line of health technology, including MRI, CT and X-ray scanners, monitors, advanced clinical software, and personal devices like electric toothbrushes and sleep apnea masks.

Defining Potential Digital Offerings

Inspired by how digital technologies can enable a healthier world, Philips is now offering integrated healthcare solutions. The company has a goal of improving the lives of three billion people a year by 2025.[10] As part of achieving that goal, the company is developing healthcare technology offerings that support individuals, clinicians, and healthcare organizations.

For example, in the consumer space, Philips's uGrow solution is an app for new parents that will provide a detailed picture of how their baby is developing. Philips's uGrow is produced from data culled from a range of connected devices, such as thermometers, scales, baby bottles, and baby monitors. The solution—a "maternity nurse in your pocket"—provides data that can also be valuable to a healthcare professional.

In the clinical space, Philips's IntelliSpace Oncology and IntelliSpace Cardiovascular offerings integrate scientific findings with patient data (such as lab and radiology results) to provide actionable insights to inform doctors' diagnoses. Physicians typically have little time to analyze what is often a massive amount of data when diagnosing a case. To streamline physicians' efforts, IntelliSpace solutions apply artificial intelligence to identify important anomalies and changes in a patient's condition (e.g., a growing tumor, a new issue with a blood vessel) and to recommend optimal therapies. Testing the new IntelliSpace algorithms on past cases revealed that, in 20 percent of the cases, doctors had recommended suboptimal treatment. Philips expects that use of these solutions will save even more lives than current approaches to medical care.

In the hospital space, Philips has developed eICU, a solution combining bedside monitors and analytics software that provides centralized, remote oversight of intensive care units. This solution helps ICU doctors and nurses prioritize urgent care cases and identify candidates for ICU release while significantly reducing workload and improving productivity.

Standardizing Enterprise Systems and Processes

To make these and other digital offerings possible, Philips embarked on a business transformation in 2011 that continues to demand senior leadership vision and commitment. Early transformation efforts focused on implementing enterprise systems to standardize three core processes: idea-to-market, for bringing a concept to market and managing the product lifecycle; market-to-order, for marketing and selling the product; and order-to-cash, for fulfilling and distributing orders, invoicing, and handling payments. These efforts have been supported by the introduction of the Philips Integrated Landscape (PIL), a technological infrastructure that has helped provide reliable transactions and data.

Philips began experimenting with using digital technologies to enhance its product offerings in late 2014. For example, Philips started using analytics and artificial intelligence to help professional caregivers interpret X-ray results. The company also developed several apps with increasing functionality to enable individuals to track results from personal devices like sleep apnea masks and electric toothbrushes.

Seeking Customer Input

Philips tested individual offerings with patients and healthcare providers to learn what they would find useful. But leaders recognized that to dramatically impact the cost and quality of healthcare, they needed to work with healthcare providers to identify game-changing solutions. Accordingly, Philips created HealthSuite Labs: stand-alone, fee-based, multi-week engagements including multi-day workshops, intended to help existing and potential healthcare clients articulate a vision and an approach for changing how they provide healthcare.

HealthSuite Lab sessions assemble cross-functional groups of leaders from Philips and a healthcare client and, in many cases, that client's stakeholders, such as patients, insurance companies, or government leaders. Lab sessions incorporate practices from design thinking and Agile development as part of a structured methodology for co-creating prototypes of integrated solutions that will improve the way care is provided.

Building Digital Platforms

As Philips was learning what solutions would benefit key customers—and change the face of healthcare—technologists were building out HealthSuite Digital Platform (HSDP) and the Connected Digital Platforms and Propositions (CDP^2) platform. These platforms are technology assets that provide repositories of data, technology, and business components (i.e., code that performs a specific activity). For every new offering, architects of these two platforms identify components that are likely to be useful for future, often unknown, offerings. They place those components in one of the repositories to facilitate reuse. Over time, Philips intends to engage with ecosystem partners who might both develop solutions and use HSDP services for their businesses. To this end, Philips has opened up HSDP to external parties via a developer portal, HSDP.io.

Changing Work

Philips's digital vision has generated an abundance of ideas for new customer offerings, some of which digitally integrate several of Philips's products, and all of which potentially will lead to a healthier world. To improve the odds that new offerings will fulfill its mission, Philips is redesigning the company to exploit its growing ability to create valuable solutions from components. Specifically, Philips is mapping out an organizational approach that distinguishes two business types: (1) component businesses that create reusable components for multiple solutions from (2) solution businesses that aggregate and integrate those components into solutions. At the executive team level, senior leaders direct resources to proposals that are most likely to lead to development of reusable components.

At Philips, the development of digital offerings now mirrors the iterative product development processes found in software companies rather than the product development processes found in consumer or engineering companies. Salespeople are also experiencing role changes. To sell new digital, integrated solutions they must interact with senior leaders at customer companies. They also must seek out new kinds of customers (e.g., insurance companies). In doing so, their roles have expanded to include not only educating customers on existing solutions, but also working with customers to identify potential new solutions.

How Do Companies Transform for Digital?

Digital business design aims to make a company agile so that it can create an innovative and constantly evolving portfolio of digital offerings in response to rapidly changing technologies and customer demands. As the Philips case shows, digital design involves significant changes to a company's people, processes, and technology. We noted that these three elements interact and that the pace of change in the digital economy means that one—and therefore all—will be changing constantly. So how do you design for digital?

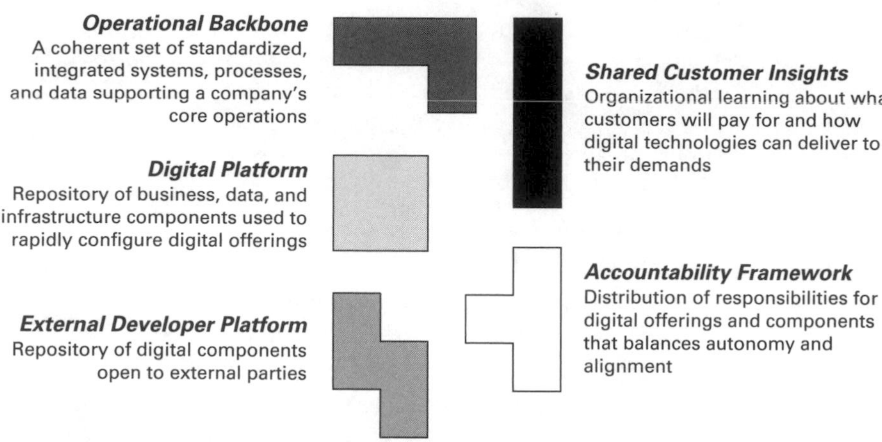
Operational Backbone
A coherent set of standardized, integrated systems, processes, and data supporting a company's core operations
Digital Platform
Repository of business, data, and infrastructure components used to rapidly configure digital offerings
External Developer Platform
Repository of digital components open to external parties
Shared Customer Insights
Organizational learning about what customers will pay for and how digital technologies can deliver to their demands
Accountability Framework
Distribution of responsibilities for digital offerings and components that balances autonomy and alignment

Figure 1.1
Five building blocks for a digital transformation

We have identified five building blocks (think of them as organizational capabilities) that help companies succeed digitally. These five building blocks enable companies to rapidly deliver innovative digital offerings. They incrementally transform companies that were not born-digital into digital companies by developing three interacting elements: (1) people who understand what needs to be done and how to do it, (2) processes that guide a company from idea through delivery to support digital offerings, and (3) technology that supports both efficient organizational processes and innovative digital offerings.

Figure 1.1 shows the five building blocks essential to digital success. We use an example from the Philips case to illustrate each building block:

- Shared customer insights: configuring people, processes, and technology to learn what customers want (e.g., Philips's understanding of customer needs gained through HealthSuite Labs)
- Operational backbone: configuring people, processes, and technology to ensure reliable, efficient core processes to support stable operations (e.g., Philips's core enterprise systems, referred to as Philips Integrated Landscape, which support standardized processes)

- Digital platform: configuring people, processes, and technology to build and use software components to configure digital offerings (e.g., Philips's HSDP and CDP[2])
- Accountability framework: configuring people, processes, and technology to ensure that individuals take responsibility for the success and evolution of digital offerings (e.g., Philips's redesign around component businesses and solution businesses)
- External developer platform: configuring people, processes, and technology to engage partners to leverage and expand their portfolio of digital offerings (e.g., Philips's HSDP.io)

The advantage of approaching digital business design as a set of building blocks is that it allows leaders to focus on specific, manageable organizational changes while implementing holistic design. This is possible because the building blocks are interdependent—making one of the building blocks stronger contributes to making the others stronger. Each building block triggers changes in people, processes, and technology in ways that make the company more agile.

Each of the building blocks requires investments of organizational resources. The companies in our research are making these investments, but they are doing so in different ways and at different times. In fact, we have no evidence of a single best template or design for your building blocks or the order in which you develop them. Indeed, our research has not found *the* optimal digital design. Leaders in the companies we've studied are making tough decisions about priorities for development of the building blocks individually and as a whole.

The next five chapters in this book detail why each building block is important and what you must do to develop it. Then, in chapter 7 we take a look at the overall digital journey. We note again that the development of the five building blocks is essential to digital success, and we show how four different companies have, in their own way, assembled their building blocks to create a digital business. In chapter 8 we discuss how companies successfully exploit the capabilities of new digital technologies, using artificial intelligence as an example. We then close the book with a list of six things companies can do to embark on a successful digital transformation.

The Call to Action

This book tells stories of a number of companies that are working aggressively to build digital building blocks and deliver digital offerings. Although we reviewed the digital efforts of nearly 200 established companies, we were not able to find many that were far along on the journey. Thus, you'll find that we rely on a fairly small set of companies to explain how companies are building their capabilities. We believe these companies represent the state of the art in digital transformations.

Transforming to become digital is risky. Companies must deliver value propositions that demand skills they have not yet acquired, processes they have not yet embedded, and technologies they have not yet implemented. Here are the key points we suggest you keep in mind:

- Becoming digital involves being inspired by the capabilities of digital technologies (think SMACIT) to develop digital offerings (information-enriched solutions that engage customers in a seamless, personalized experience). *How can ubiquitous data, unlimited connectivity, and massive processing power expand your customer value propositions?*
- Developing a constantly evolving portfolio of digital offerings requires business agility. Established companies are not designed for agility. For the most part, they have been structured for efficiency. *Can you make changes to your people, processes, and technology that don't start with restructuring?*
- To design for digital, companies can focus on five building blocks, each configuring people, processes, and technology for the rapid delivery of digital offerings. *Which building blocks do you have in place? Which will be particularly challenging for your company?*
- Digital business design is a senior executive responsibility. *Who is taking charge of digital business design in your company?*

Perhaps some established companies will be able to sustain success without transforming to become digital. More likely, mapping out a future based on that hope is even riskier than the transformation we are describing. To minimize your risk of digital disruption, you need to design a business that can respond to unknown future technologies and customer demands. Designing your business for digital takes time. You'd better start now. We hope this book will help guide your journey.

2 Building Shared Customer Insights

According to various history books, Christopher Columbus set out in 1492 to find a new route to the Indies from Europe. His actions were driven by a bold vision with significant risks and uncertainties, but he (and his financial backers, King Ferdinand and Queen Isabella) believed the potential payoff justified the risk.

It so happens that Columbus did not make it to the Indies. He ran into the Bahamas on his westward journey. When he did so, he did not think he'd failed. Nor did he set out to find a way around the Bahamas so that he could achieve his original objective. Instead, Columbus claimed his discovered lands for the Crown of Castile and declared his mission a success.[1] It is now well established that Columbus's riches were ill begotten, so we are not applauding his behavior. But his story is interesting because, even though he never reached the intended destination, his vision took him somewhere worth going.

Companies could have a similar experience on their digital journeys. As they attempt to imagine value propositions based on the capabilities of digital technologies, leaders are navigating uncharted waters. Those waters are rough! Digital technologies, customer demands, and business competition are all rapidly changing, making outcomes unpredictable and success fleeting. Companies will need to adapt to the realities they encounter and the opportunities they find.

Companies Learn What Makes a Viable Digital Offering

One problem you're likely to encounter as you commit to developing digital offerings is that it's hard to know exactly which digital offerings represent a great opportunity for your company. You need to start developing digital offerings now so you can figure out your opportunities—and fend off disruptors. A successful digital offering leverages the capabilities of digital technologies to provide a solution to a problem or issue that a customer invariably hasn't articulated. It represents the intersection between what customers desire (even if they don't know it yet) and what digital technologies make possible. See figure 2.1 for a representation of a digital offering.

Finding the point of intersection between what a company can do with digital technologies and what a customer wants is challenging for two reasons. First, most companies have little experience imagining what solutions they might develop with digital technologies. They are still learning what ubiquitous data, unlimited connectivity, and massive processing power make possible.

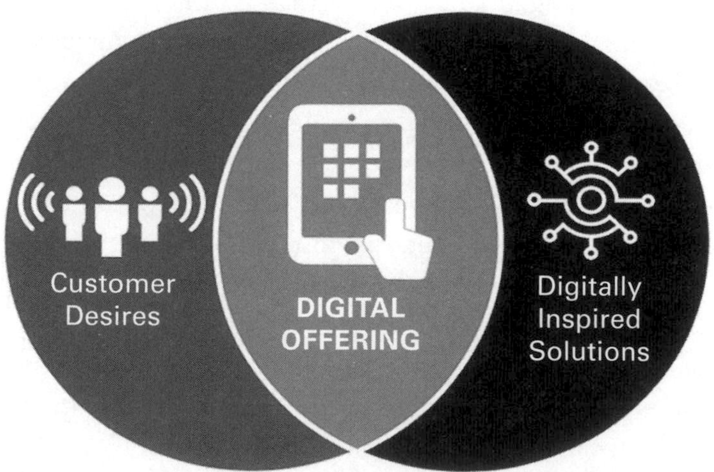

Figure 2.1
Digital offering: customer desires intersect with solutions

Second, customers often can't imagine what they want until they have it. Steve Jobs famously declared that he didn't ask customers what they wanted because he knew better than they did. The iPhone thus emerged from out-of-the-box thinking, as did Uber, Facebook, and Airbnb, rather than from resounding customer demand. Companies trying to solve customer problems have limited direction as to what a customer will find valuable.

In theory, the number of potential digitally inspired customer solutions is nearly infinite (a typical MBA class can propose dozens of ideas in a single class session). In practice, most possible solutions would never find a customer base. Thus, identifying solutions that will generate genuine customer enthusiasm (in the form of willingness to pay) is not a trivial task. If you want to deliver valuable digital offerings, you'll need to aggressively seek out the intersection of customer desires and digitally inspired solutions.

The experiences of starry-eyed college students are actually relevant to companies embarking on digital transformations. College students have a propensity for dreaming up digital offerings that crusty old academics can't imagine will attract customers. Indeed, the crusty academics are often right. When students hit the sidewalks to try to sell their ideas, they often get a quizzical look from a potential customer who doesn't see the value. In some cases, however, students' proposals spark creative ideas in the minds of bemused potential customers, who might respond: "I'm not interested in that, but let me tell you what I would find valuable." The students are back in business, flush with customer insights. With enough iterations of such a feedback cycle, students may find the sweet spot where what they can develop intersects with what customers will buy.

This iterative development process is the norm. Consider, for example, that Airbnb grew out of the belief that people would pay to sleep on an air mattress on a stranger's floor.[2] Similarly, Instagram started as an app for checking in and hanging out with friends (and sharing pictures) that proved too complicated to use.[3] Twitter's founders first tried a podcasting platform, Odeo, which Apple made obsolete.[4] Even AUDI had to kill off its "share a car among five friends" app before rolling out successful mobility services.[5] For new and old companies alike, digital offerings are born out of iterating with an idea until it finds the sweet spot in figure 2.1.

Experiments Create Shared Customer Insights

Iterating to find the intersection of what digital technologies make possible with what customers will buy is a test-and-learn process.[6] Digital offerings are well suited to rapid test and learn because they are software based. Software coders can develop a minimum viable product (MVP), release it to customers or a test group, and get immediate feedback. Based on the feedback, a company can quickly enhance or discard the product.

Companies seeking to develop viable digital offerings adopt this approach. They encourage widespread experimentation through events like hackathons and other competitions, through special funding opportunities like an internal kickstarter.com or "shark tank" proposal review process, and through new organizational units like innovation labs and digital business units. They learn about customer desires by mapping out customer journeys, by co-innovating with key customers, by releasing code and monitoring customer feedback.

Of course, such widespread innovation could simply waste resources on pointless experiments. Companies can counter that risk by insisting on small experiments that quickly produce measurable outcomes. Any experiment that doesn't quickly generate customer enthusiasm can be abandoned, while those with the most potential can be cultivated. This is hard to do. People with an idea want it to succeed, so they will be tempted to tweak an unsuccessful idea rather than abandon it.

Learning from experiments depends on recognizing what isn't working and shifting resources to something that might be more successful. As Frans van Houten, CEO of Philips, notes:

> When we make big, $50 million mistakes, it is usually because we are killing something too late. It's the typical innovator's problem.

Whether an experiment succeeds or fails, building a successful digital business requires accumulating learning about how the company can use digital technologies to address customer needs. In big companies, accumulating such learning is only half the challenge. Individuals and business units must share their learning. Otherwise, multiple people within a company may invest in similar experiments to learn the same lesson.

Successful digital businesses have a natural ability to experiment with potential offerings so they can learn what they can do and what customers want. They have configured people, processes, and technologies to incorporate digital offering experiments into their DNA. In doing so, they are developing a building block we call *shared customer insights,* defined as organizational learning about what customers will pay for and how digital technologies can deliver to customer demands.

Schneider Electric, which has transformed multiple times since its founding in 1836 as a producer of iron and steel, offers an example of a company accumulating shared customer insights to deliver new customer value propositions.

Building Shared Customer Insights at Schneider Electric

Since around 2014, Schneider Electric has been on a digital transformation that has made it a leader in energy management and automation in homes, buildings, data centers, infrastructure, and industrial settings.[7] With a global presence in over 100 countries and 2017 revenues of €25B, Schneider is providing integrated efficiency solutions that combine energy equipment, automation, and software.

In the ten years prior to its digital transformation, Schneider had acquired over 200 companies and brands. These acquisitions enabled the company to expand its energy equipment products and solutions to include:

- Power distribution products
- Metering products that measure energy consumption
- Building management systems and security
- Data center physical infrastructure

- Grid infrastructure management systems
- Intelligent energy management solutions

Like its competitors, in its early adoption of sensing technology and the Internet of Things (IoT), Schneider provided remote monitoring of large electrical equipment (e.g., switches, circuit breakers, transformers). But this remote monitoring was largely a device-by-device service: when a product malfunctioned, both the customer and salesperson received an alert indicating that the equipment potentially needed to be replaced. This remote monitoring originally was more of a sales tool than a customer service.

Inspired by the capabilities of IoT, Schneider's leaders believed sensors and connectivity could provide customers with far more than an alert that equipment was failing. In particular, business leaders proposed that sophisticated analysis of integrated sensor data could help customers become much more energy efficient. Accordingly, the company adopted a mission of delivering solutions that ensure that "Life Is On™ for everyone, everywhere, and at every moment." This mission is a commitment to provide customers with reliable, cost-effective energy management.

Early Experiments

Initially, business units experimented individually with new customer solutions aligned with the company's vision and burgeoning digital strategy. Product development staff in the business units worked with customers to understand their expectations, needs, and challenges and, in turn, identified digital enhancements to products. Schneider's IoT Technology Platform Vice President Michael MacKenzie described how individual lines of business funded these early efforts and ideas proliferated:

> At the start, the businesses owned their product roadmaps and therefore determined their needs: local initiatives, local success, and failures, sometimes. They were making decisions and learning in a microcosm.

These early experiments generated some successes. As far back as 2012, Schneider's IT division had introduced its Data Center Infrastructure Management (DCIM) solution, called StruxureWare™. DCIM offered an integrated set of products, solutions, software, and services across a data center's physical infrastructure, including power, cooling, energy management, and remote monitoring. According to Schneider, 40% of the ongoing cost of managing a data center is energy, so this kind of offering possessed a strong use case for energy management solutions. And because they were, by nature, comfortable with software-based solutions, data center customers were eager to acquire and use this new solution.

In general, however, the company's initial business unit–driven approach to developing digital offerings did not deliver the expected results. Prototypes built within business units were expensive and prone to scalability and security issues. The proliferation of local offerings was not building either significant new revenue streams or reusable strategic capabilities. Schneider's IoT & Digital Offers Executive Vice President Cyril Perducat said of this initial approach,

> Everyone across the company is trying to reinvent digital for our products, so everybody is establishing partnerships with different start-ups offering all types of technology innovations. But this results in multiplication of partnerships, multiplication of cloud providers, multiplication of connectivity protocols, anything you can imagine in digital.

To address these issues, Schneider took advantage of SMACIT technologies, such as mobility, cloud, analytics, IoT, and cybersecurity, to bolster shared digital capabilities for all its businesses. Cyril Perducat, head of IoT & Digital Offers for Schneider Electric, took responsibility for seeking business opportunities to create new offerings that leveraged these shared capabilities. He found that business leaders were reluctant to shift their offerings to the shared infrastructure, so he created an internal Digital Services Factory (DSF) to ensure that the businesses saw increased benefits and lower risks when they did so.

Formalizing Learning and Engaging Customers

Perducat's team partners with the business units (and with virtual teams from an ecosystem of external partners) to bring together capabilities to generate ideas for digital offerings within the context of key market trends and needs. Some ideas come directly from an interested customer, while others come from business leaders responding to reported customer needs, problems, pain points, and desires. More recently, the company has started to surface new opportunities from data insights based on how customers are using their digital services.

The DSF team escorts concepts for digital offerings through four stages: ideation, incubation, industrialization, and run and scale. In the ideation phase, they review new ideas to identify recurring and similar concepts, because those ideas, if applied by multiple business units, are likely to deliver greater value. Product teams engage key customers early in the ideation phase to learn the viability of a concept. The Digital Services Factory team quickly stops those ideas that do not appear to have a viable business case. Meanwhile, the company assigns business product owners to the most promising ideas.

If a concept moves to the industrialization stage, Schneider typically requires that a customer fund a pilot, thus increasing the likelihood that initial customer enthusiasm will convert into revenues. IoT Strategy & Business Design Vice President Carlos Javaroni explained how, in this phase, cross-functional teams work jointly with the customer to ensure that the offering delivers on the customer value proposition and that the customer sees it:

> The voice of the customer is the critical place to begin. Understanding the business problem we are trying to solve informs us about the appetite for the solution. In several cases, we have received very positive customer feedback, but that's not necessarily enough for them to spend money on it. Therefore, we keep our customers at the center of our co-innovation.

Some innovations add digital features to existing products. For those, industrialization involves finding customers interested in the new features and value. The existing product sales staff will take on that responsibility. For more strategic energy management solutions, Schneider has found that its usual customer contact isn't the right person to make the purchasing decision. For these so-called "C-level" offerings, Schneider is developing a small team of more experienced and highly specialized salespeople.

Schneider has found that customers tend to adopt C-level offerings incrementally, as they learn how to benefit from them. Thus, the specialized salespeople can be valued members of product development teams, helping to incrementally develop offerings customers want at the pace they want them.

Accelerating Product Development

To accumulate shared customer insights, Schneider has created a new development process for its digital offerings. The company's traditional product development involved lengthy, rigorous research and development followed by prolonged rollouts of important innovations. In contrast, the digital offering product life cycle, driven by the DSF, starts with an identified customer need; proceeds through development of a minimum viable product that customers test and use; and then enters a stage of continuous improvement, expansion, and development of related offerings.

Schneider has partnered with a variety of best-in-breed technology companies to apply more iterative development approaches and co-innovation. This has involved abandoning legacy IT methodologies and pre-digital product R&D approaches for purposes of developing digital offerings. As a result, Schneider has collapsed the time from ideation to industrialization from two or three years to just a year. Chief Digital Officer Hervé Coureil described how combining different approaches has improved product development:

> R&D will take time to release a product, because it has to be more than perfect. And with good reason. Our products have safety functions. Then you have the world of software, which says, "Okay. Let's experiment. Let's iterate. Let's do it like startups do. Let's give them a Minimum Viable Product." Connecting the two approaches is one of the interesting challenges of business leaders.

As it gradually builds shared customer insights, Schneider has started generating revenues and profits from new digital offerings. In 2018, Schneider had around 40 digital offerings, including digital services for asset management (e.g., predictive maintenance), energy resource management for C-level business forecasting and budgeting, and consolidated remote monitoring of specialized machine fleets. Another 20 offerings were nearing roll-out.

Designing for Shared Customer Insights

As the Schneider example suggests, digital companies develop an ability to learn what their customers will find valuable. The essence of designing for shared customer insights is creating roles and processes that help a company find the intersection between what solutions it can deliver and what solutions the customer wants, as suggested by figure 2.1. Because of uncertainty around both how customers want to be engaged and what customers want, digital offering development involves constantly testing the viability of ideas. This process is sometimes referred to as discovery-driven planning.[8] Companies with a shared customer insight capability have built up a knowledge base about the problems, inconveniences, and desires of their current or potential customers, and that allows them to more quickly identify and seize opportunities.

Schneider Electric and other leading companies have adopted a number of design practices supporting the accumulation of shared customer insights. Our research found that these practices are associated with increased revenues from digital offerings:[9]

- A high-level digital vision for new customer value
- A constant flow of digital experiments that test how digital technologies can deliver customer value
- Tightly integrated product development, sales, and service processes
- Customer co-creation of digital offerings
- Formalized sharing of learning across the enterprise

High-Level Vision

Schneider Electric's vision of providing intelligent energy management solutions guides choices about what experiments to pursue. Similarly, Philips's stated vision to improve healthcare outcomes at lower cost and USAA's vision of ensuring the financial security of its members establish general parameters for experiments of interest. As a result, these visions limit the odds that experiments will simply distract a company from strategic pursuits.

It is worth noting that while we call these visions "digital" (because they are inspired by digital technologies), they are, in fact, these companies' overall business visions. In a digital economy, a digital vision is the business vision.

Many early visions provide only a rough idea of potential customer digital offerings. For example, CEMEX, a global cement manufacturer based in Mexico, intends to create a customer experience that will make the entire construction industry more efficient. It kicked off the effort to deliver on that vision by developing a digital platform called CEMEX Go, which provides visibility into a building contractor's (i.e., the customer's) transactions and order status through a mobile app. CEMEX will learn how to make the construction industry more efficient as it experiments with new functionality and solutions around CEMEX Go.[10]

A pharmaceutical company that has traditionally developed and sold drugs now imagines a broader vision as a disease expert. This vision encourages experiments focused on preventing, diagnosing, and treating illnesses apart from drug development. In shifting its vision from providing drugs to fighting diseases, the company expects to take advantage of massive amounts of data it already owns or can easily access. This will surely lead to new value propositions delivered by a more expansive set of services that could include lifestyle changes, diet changes, or gene therapies in addition to drugs. The revenue model for such offerings will surely differ from drugs. How will the company learn what it can do that customers will pay for? By experimenting.

As companies build customer insights, their visions are likely to evolve. For example, the Singapore-based financial services company DBS Bank started pursuing its goal to be the "Asian bank of choice" in 2010. By 2014, the company was "making banking invisible." Its vision in 2018 was "making banking joyful," with the branding position "Live More, Bank Less." DBS's evolving vision first helped position DBS as the bank of choice for customers and employees. Building on what it learned, it has disrupted banking in India by launching an entirely digital mobile-only bank there.[11] In 2017 and 2018 DBS began offering car, property, and electricity marketplaces on the DBS website. In short, digital visions direct experiments. In turn, experiments invariably reshape a vision.

Constant Flow of Experiments

Although no company has unlimited capacity for experiments, conducting more experiments generally leads to more learning. Schneider manages the capacity issue by quickly assessing the potential of ideas through the development of minimum viable products and discarding those ideas that aren't resonating with customers.

DBS Bank has dispersed responsibility for digital innovation throughout the company. DBS, which is the biggest bank in Southeast Asia (in terms of assets under management), provides a full range of financial services to 9 million customers in 18 markets. In 2015, its 22,000 employees were concurrently running 1,000 small experiments throughout the bank. Some of these experiments were quickly abandoned; others evolved into digital offerings or features for customers.

To generate shared customer insights, DBS stimulates idea generation and idea testing with techniques such as internal crowdsourcing, customer experience labs, hackathons, external partnering, nurturing of fintech startups, and technology scanning. One highly touted initiative partners senior leaders with young technology staff in hackathons. The company has observed that this exercise is valuable for helping senior leaders recognize the possibilities that digital technologies create while focusing younger staff on important business problems.[12]

A major source of ideas worth testing at DBS is examination of the customer's journey, which involves mapping the full experience of customers as they interact with the company. Designers attempt to get inside the mind of the customer—to feel like they *are* the customer—at moments such as when a customer decides to use a DBS product. Designers sometimes create a "pretend" customer, giving the person a name, age, and occupation, and take this customer through the journey of applying for, say, a mortgage or credit card, to understand what that customer is going through. They then consider what the customer is thinking, what emotions they are experiencing, what their concerns are. Given those insights, they try to improve the customer experience.[13]

One member of the top management committee of each business unit at DBS heads a "Customer Journey Experience" team, as a peer to (and working with) the product heads, functional heads, and country heads of that business. Customer Journey Experience teams work with product teams to ensure that "journey-thinking" inspires experiments.

DBS's pursuit of customer insights and constant flow of experiments is paying off. In 2016, and again in 2018, DBS was named the "World's Best Digital Bank" by *Euromoney*. In 2018 *Global Finance Magazine* also named DBS "Best Bank in the World."[14]

Toyota Motor North America (TMNA) has also introduced a variety of approaches to fostering digital experiments.[15] When Zack Hicks, now the company's chief digital officer, was CIO, he introduced an

Innovation Fair at which employees shared their innovative ideas with others in the company and competed for funding and the prestige of seeing their ideas move forward. Losing teams could also apply for funding from a variety of sources. This concept has been absorbed into global innovation fairs at Toyota Motor Corporation.

The innovation fair is just one way that TMNA encourages experimentation and innovation. For example, TMNA has an iCouncil that acts as a polite "shark tank." iCouncil members, who have director-level business positions (and budgets), might help the owner of an idea develop a business case, authorize funding from a director's budget or a special CIO fund, or team up an innovator with an IT person who could develop a simple app.

TMNA has also established The Garage, a small area within IT where two contractors provide up to 30 hours of development time to individuals who want to try out a new idea. The Garage allows people to circumvent typical funding processes to create a prototype that might demonstrate the viability of a concept. The Garage also offers equipment like iPads and server space to individuals who want to experiment with an idea. Promising ideas can be shopped around to a specific business unit or entered into the Innovation Fair.

Finally, TMNA IT developed a Kickstarter type of application where individuals can post ideas for innovations and receive feedback. This app is particularly good for those ideas that are creative but too raw for testing. A user can share the idea on a forum where others can respond with a thumbs-up or -down and with suggestions that might help advance the concept.

Most of the experiments that emerge from TMNA's initiatives target the customer experience. Some are relatively simple and quickly developed, such as an app that helps customers interact efficiently with dealers after they have started to configure their preferred vehicle online. In some cases, however, TMNA's small experiments lead to changes in products or kick off new offerings. Experiments have led, for example, to innovations in the application of telecommunications and satellite systems for in-car safety, GPS, and entertainment services.

Tightly Integrated Product Development, Sales, and Service Processes

A number of business leaders in our research expressed surprise about how long it can take customers to warm up to compelling value propositions. A new value proposition invariably requires a customer to act differently—to disrupt a power structure, shift expertise, or respond to new data. As noted above, Schneider Electric found that it needed a different sales force to sell and inform its "C-level" intelligent energy management solutions.

ING Direct Spain relies on cross-functional teams to ensure that new offerings address a customer's needs end-to-end.[16] Functions like product management, marketing, operations, IT, credit risk, and operational risk work together at a very early stage of product definition. The benefit of these cross-functional teams is to bring together different perspectives that encourage mutual challenging. This mutual challenging mitigates the risk of designing offerings that the company cannot afford to support or that create customer hassles rather than a great experience. This helps ING Direct Spain limit business complexity. Werner Zippold, former COO of ING Direct Spain, explained the value of airing very different perspectives before putting a new product into production:

> Any idea that survives that sort of challenging has a certain guarantee that it's well thought through in terms of how you actually handle the operational complexity later, because you have operations and IT people actually contributing in the definition. And they can offer solutions or twist the way we do things to make it a lot simpler. You need to be able to challenge the business side: "From my perspective, are you really sure that the value added justifies that increase in complexity?"

Exposing potential offerings to both front office and back office experts surfaces complexity and has given ING Direct Spain more manageable systems and processes, which supports reuse as the company develops digital offerings.

Customer Co-creation of Digital Offerings

Schneider's approach to building customer insights involves working directly with customers early and often. Digital innovations are brilliant only if customers are willing to buy them. Every company has made false assumptions about what customers might want. A company with a shared customer insights asset can quickly identify and correct those false assumptions.

Philips's attempts to redefine healthcare are heavily dependent on what customers (including healthcare providers, insurers, and individual consumers) are ready to buy and use. Customers have habits and they are not always willing to change those habits, even when the benefits of doing so seem obvious. Philips's efforts are further hampered by industry complexity.

A consistent challenge is that many healthcare improvements help one party but negatively impact another. For example, insurers want their patients to recover quickly from surgery, but for hospitals, empty beds reduce revenues. Similarly, helping individuals stay healthy is a universal desire. Nonetheless, insurance companies are not always willing to pick up incremental costs for keeping people healthy, even though such costs will invariably be lower than treating a preventable illness or condition.

The complexities and uncertainties around the development of healthcare solutions led Philips to invest substantial resources in customer co-creation efforts such as their HealthSuite Lab workshops. The intention of these multi-session HealthSuite Lab workshops is to learn about customers' most pressing problems and to figure out how to solve them—in other words, to learn what customers are likely willing to pay for. As Manu Varma, Business Leader for Wellcentive and Hospital to Home at Philips, noted, "We don't always know what customers' challenges are. They don't know what they want." HealthSuite Labs is a consultative process designed to enlighten both sides.

When embarking on a HealthSuite Labs engagement, the customer (usually a healthcare provider) and Philips agree to solve a complex healthcare challenge jointly. To do so, HealthSuite Labs sessions typically bring together providers (e.g., hospital managers, physicians, nurses), patients, and payers (insurance companies, government agencies). In total, a HealthSuite Labs session can include 12 to 40 people, many of whom are not regularly in a position to talk with each other. Mark van Meggelen, Business Leader of Healthcare Information and Connected Care for Philips in Benelux, describes the impact of participating in HealthSuite Labs as follows:

> In the past, we had talked a lot about patients, but I never actually met a patient until we started pioneering HealthSuite Labs. It made me humble, because of the burden the disease entails for patients. The way they are supported is far from optimal.

The multidisciplinary and collaborative approach of HealthSuite Labs allows teams to tackle difficult healthcare issues; their proposed solutions aim to improve the overall healthcare system rather than improve the processes or outcomes of a single stakeholder. For example, a HealthSuite Labs engagement could lead to redesign of reimbursement schemes so that all parties profit and are incentivized to do what is best from the perspective of system-wide outcomes and costs.

Formalized Sharing of Learning across the Enterprise

Schneider has folded its Digital Services Team into a Digital Business Unit reporting directly to the CEO. This unit owns responsibility for accumulating and sharing learning about customers and digital technologies. This shared learning helps build functionality into the Schneider EcoStruxure platform that supports digital offerings. It also provides insights into which proposed experiments are most promising.

Decades of research on product development have demonstrated the risks of isolated innovation. In particular, innovation, while essential to vibrant business models, can nonetheless lead to non-value-adding business complexity.[17] This is what happens if experiments take place locally and the learning is not shared. Companies will miss opportunities to integrate data, products, and services across product lines or business units that can lead to new customer value propositions.

Some companies have created centers of excellence, where experts can exploit learning from other parts of the company. For example, Ferrovial, a Spanish infrastructure company with 70,000 employees, has created an innovation center staffed with 25 people who help teams develop competitive bids for new business by identifying relevant prior solutions, potential third-party partners, or solutions that exist in the marketplace. The innovation center attempts to solve any problem that will obstruct development of innovative bids. In doing so, the center reuses expertise that might otherwise remain local.[18]

Alternatively, some companies push innovation expertise and tools out into the business. At DBS, the Customer Journey Experience teams help others in the business learn how to answer questions about customer journeys, often hand in hand with similarly distributed analytics teams.

Creating a Culture for Shared Customer Insights

Driven by the fear of digital disruption and/or the thrill of digital greatness, companies are designing organizational roles and processes for accumulating insights on both the capabilities of digital technologies and the interests of customers. In doing so, they are building an organizational asset that positions them for digital success.

Building this asset involves disrupting established management practices and individual habits. In other words, it forces a change in corporate culture. Taking an iterative test-and-learn approach to developing offerings will be a foreign concept to almost anyone who has risen to the top of an established company. For example, pharmaceutical companies have 10-year development cycles; auto manufacturers often take 5 years to develop, test, and roll out new products. These long cycles involve huge allocations of resources. They are "big bet" strategic initiatives.

Most digital innovations are much smaller bets. A few of those smaller bets could become very big deals, but most will be discarded. Imagine the carnival game where each player can bet on any horse until the race begins. Once the race starts, the bettor just hopes to win. Conducting digital experiments is like betting a tiny amount on all the horses at the gate and then having the option to increase any bet at various points during the race. There is no need to make a big bet until the winner is almost certain. The shared customer insights building block allows companies to place their bets exactly this way.

Getting Customer Insights Right

Digital offerings must find the point of intersection between what digital technologies can do to redefine your company's value proposition and what your customers will value. To find that sweet spot, you'll need to configure people, processes, and technology in ways that encourage a test-and-learn approach to developing digital offerings. People must learn new habits guided by new processes and enabled by new technologies and data. To support your efforts to build shared customer insights, this chapter developed the following key points:

- Shared customer insights emerge from constantly conducting experiments that test what digital offerings the company can develop and what customers value. *What mechanisms (labs, contests, venture funding sources, innovation roles, customer engagement processes) can you develop to encourage employees to test, learn, and share ideas for digital offerings?*
- A test-and-learn environment requires an evidence-based culture—people who hypothesize, experiment, collect data, measure results, and use outcomes to guide next steps. *Do you have an evidence-based culture? What can you do to increase your company's ability to test and learn?*
- Digital experiments should be guided by a vision, but your vision will evolve based on the outcomes of your experiments. This is how you will zero in on successful digital offerings. *Is everyone in your company aware of the value proposition you envision for your (digital) company? Does everyone know the successes and failures you've encountered in your attempts to deliver that value proposition?*

Shared customer insights are valuable for identifying early digital offerings. They are just as important for constantly enhancing and evolving your portfolio of digital offerings over time. The habits you create for shared customer insights are a long-term asset. They will make you more agile, and they will help you focus on critical requirements for your other building blocks.

3 Building an Operational Backbone

Both facts and folklore herald the Titanic as the most remarkable, lavish, exciting passenger vessel of its time. The ship offered an incomparable customer experience. Designers and builders had tended to many details both for safety (including watertight compartments and remotely activated watertight doors) and for comfort (such as swimming pool, gymnasium, libraries, high-class restaurants, and opulent cabins). This is a ship you wanted to be on. Until it sank.

As companies set out on their digital journeys, they will be seeking new, rather remarkable, value propositions. It's an exciting prospect. But leaders must ask an important question as they start their digital journeys: How do we avoid operational issues that could sink our digital efforts?

Digitized ≠ Digital

As we've already noted, digital companies deliver digital offerings. In developing digital offerings, business leaders apply digital technologies to create customer solutions. Digital technologies, however, can have just as big an impact on existing operations as they do on new value propositions.

We distinguish these two potential impacts of digital technologies as the difference between digitized and digital. Digitizing with digital technologies involves enhancing business processes and operations with SMACIT and related technologies. For example, Internet of Things technologies can automate support of distributed equipment or operations; mobile computing can create a seamless employee experience;

artificial intelligence can help automate repetitive administrative processes. These applications of digital technology can certainly benefit a company, but they digitize a company; they do not make it digital.

In contrast, digital expands and accelerates innovation. When companies become digital, they apply SMACIT and related technologies to deliver digital offerings.

Digitization enhances operational excellence; digital enhances the customer value proposition. It's important not to confuse the two. Business executives who think they are leading a digital transformation when they are, in fact, digitizing may achieve operational excellence on an outdated value proposition. This may elevate competitiveness in the short term, but it's not likely to lead to digital success. Consider the limitation of being the best taxi company in town when Uber and Lyft arrived on the scene.

Sadly, however, this does not mean that established companies can abandon the pursuit of operational excellence in favor of digital innovation. In a world of ubiquitous data, unlimited connectivity, and massive processing power, there is little room for human intervention. The speed of digital business means that employees don't have time to mess around with dysfunctional operational processes. People have work to do, decisions to make, ideas to explore. Systems, processes and data must make it easy for customers and employees to accomplish what they are trying to do. Leaders can't waste bandwidth putting out fires. They must spend their time gaining new insights and converting those insights into action.

Operational excellence has shifted from being a good idea to a "must have." Digitization was the goal of prior business transformations, for example, in enterprise resource planning (ERP) implementations. Now it is a prerequisite to digital transformation.

Operational Excellence Is Table Stakes

To understand the importance of digitization—and the resulting operational excellence—for digital businesses, start by trying to imagine how successful Amazon would be if most of its packages did not arrive on time. Or imagine Uber's success if its customer payment system went down every other week.

The need for speed requires companies to be highly efficient, to minimize time and cost. Consequently, operational excellence is no longer a potential source of competitive advantage. As a poker player would say, it's table stakes.

To be sure, becoming operationally excellent is more easily said than done. Most big companies have operated as business or functional silos for many years. Business leaders created the systems, data, and processes they needed to accomplish their objectives within their silos. In doing so, they often failed to consider how their systems and processes might eventually need to coordinate with other parts of the business. When they later recognized integration requirements, leaders often responded by tweaking systems and processes to achieve an immediate objective. Over time, narrowly focused systems and processes and the quick fixes applied to them produced costly combinations of automated and manual processes and unreliable data. (See figure 3.1 for a visual description of the problem.)

As a rule, companies have enlisted people, in a variety of roles, to address the need for linking together local systems and processes and extracting meaningful data. As reflected in figure 3.1, these people

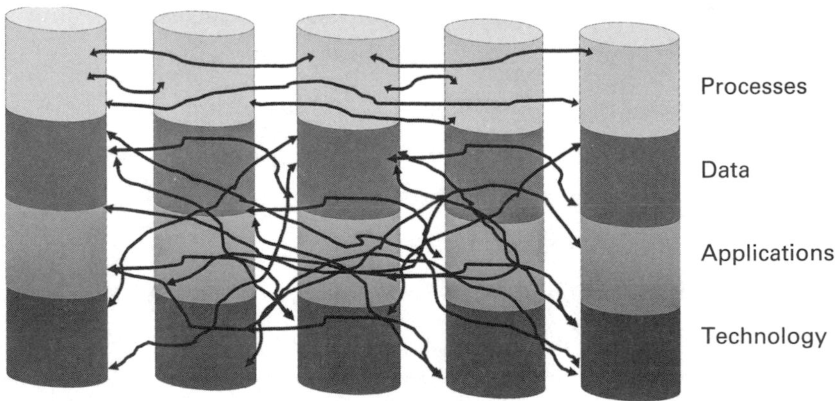

Figure 3.1
Siloed systems, processes, and data

"wire" together individual siloed systems, processes, and data in a variety of ways. For example, they (1) dump data from multiple silos into a single spreadsheet; (2) rely on the IT unit to develop one-off links to data in other systems; (3) insert manual processes between two automated processes to make them look end-to-end. We have tended to view the people creating these linkages as heroes; they have kept businesses afloat. But the net effect of their efforts—coupled with the systems they use—is to create such a complex operational environment that their companies are slow, inefficient, and high-risk.

Digital businesses will not long survive processes that rely on individual heroes. To satisfy the demands of, say, a typical user of an app, mobile transactions must be reliable and seamless. This means that, to play in the digital economy, companies need to replace their dysfunctional systems and processes with an operational backbone.

Digital Business Is Built on an Operational Backbone

An *operational backbone* is a coherent set of enterprise systems, data, and processes supporting a company's core operations. The backbone replaces the messy legacy systems, processes, and data generated by siloed business units with standardized and shared systems, processes, and data. Figure 3.2 depicts the operational backbone.

An operational backbone contributes to business success by ensuring reliable, stable, secure operations. Specifically, it does four things:

1. Supports seamless end-to-end transaction processing.
2. Provides reliable, accessible master data (i.e., a single source of truth).
3. Provides visibility into transactions and other core processes.
4. Automates repetitive business processes.

The benefits of an operational backbone are substantial. Because it eliminates—or significantly reduces—non-value-adding variability in a company's systems, processes, and data, it contributes to profitability, customer satisfaction, and innovativeness. This positions a company for digital business. In fact, our research shows that companies

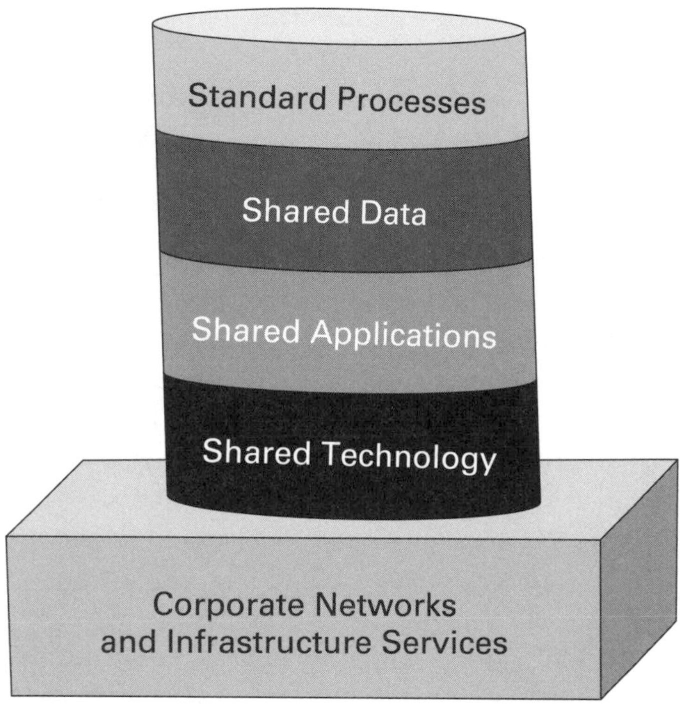

Figure 3.2
Operational backbone

with an operational backbone—companies that exhibit the above characteristics—are more agile and innovative than their competitors.[1]

> Companies with an effective operational backbone are 2.5 times as agile (measured as reusing services in developing new offerings) and 44% more innovative (measured as percentage of revenue from new offerings) than companies without an operational backbone.[2]

Take, for example, Nordstrom, a North American fashion retailer. In the highly competitive retail industry, Nordstrom took an early lead in offering online and digital services, because its operational backbone allowed buyers, supply chain managers, and even salespeople to see what was in inventory and where any given inventory item was located. That extraordinary transparency gave salespeople the power to move product at will, thereby providing the convenient, personalized service the company promised. Today that transparency allows online customers to order any item in any Nordstrom warehouse or store and to move seamlessly between in-store and online services.[3] While Nordstrom's backbone was supporting its digital services, a European retailer was frustrating customers with a "click-and-collect" offering that sometimes falsely told customers they could pick up their online purchase at a local store. Customers could arrive at their local store and learn their purchased item wasn't available. Nordstrom had digitized; the European retailer had not.

CEMEX, the global cement company, has a highly touted operational backbone it refers to as the CEMEX Way. CEMEX introduced the CEMEX Way—an approach to building, implementing, and constantly improving standardized systems and business processes across its geographically dispersed businesses—in the mid-1990s. The CEMEX Way gave CEMEX the ability to constantly improve business systems and processes enterprise-wide. It also allowed the company to quickly integrate a series of acquisitions over the next 15 years.[4]

More recently, CEMEX has found that its globally standardized processes and operational efficiencies have enabled it to shrink the time between concept and delivery of CEMEX Go, its digital platform that serves as a foundation for digital offerings. Initially rolled out in Mexico and the United States, CEMEX Go is leveraging the company's operational backbone as it rapidly adds functionality.

Kaiser Permanente, an integrated healthcare services provider serving 10 million people in the US, built an operational backbone around the implementation of an electronic medical records system.[5] By ensuring the integration and accuracy of each individual's medical information, Kaiser has been able to provide high quality care to individuals across its many facilities and providers. That ability has contributed to Kaiser's industry-high customer satisfaction ratings.[6] In addition, the company's operational backbone positioned the company to rapidly implement its mobile app. Soon thereafter Kaiser started to create offerings to fulfill its vision of fostering patient-provider collaboration.

Many business leaders were persuaded long ago that something like an operational backbone would be valuable. Thus, many companies have been attempting to clean up messy legacy systems for years. Digital transformations are creating an urgency to build an operational backbone. Our research found that an operational backbone, like shared customer insight, is an essential building block in a digital transformation. Or, to put it another way, not having an operational backbone is a huge impediment to digital success.

> 44% of executives in established companies identified the operational backbone as "the one building block that is currently the biggest obstacle to digital transformation."[7]

Most established companies have been trying to build and enhance an operational backbone for many years. Typically, these attempts have centered on implementation of enterprise systems like enterprise resource planning systems (ERPs), customer relationship management systems (CRMs), core banking engines, or electronic medical records systems. The LEGO Group offers an example of a company that successfully built an operational backbone that supports operational excellence and positions the company for becoming digital.

The LEGO Group: Building an Operational Backbone

When Jørgen Vig Knudstorp took over the reins of the LEGO Group in 2004, the company was near bankruptcy.[8] Concerns about consumers' changing tastes had given rise to massive innovation unrelated to LEGO's star product—the LEGO brick. The company had moved into children's clothing, television, and video games, and it had opened a number of theme parks. In trying to diversify, the LEGO Group had grown the number of SKUs (stock-keeping units, i.e., unique items available for sale) from 6,000 in 1997 to over 14,000 by 2004. This diverse product portfolio entailed complex and expensive production processes. Production was rigid and slow, and many of the LEGO Group's new product launches and innovations failed.

As he took the reins of the struggling company, Knudstorp quickly identified supply chain issues as a competitive disadvantage:

> One of the things that dawned on me when I arrived at the LEGO Group was that basically you have an allocation problem. You are producing 100,000 components every minute, twenty-four hours a day, 365 days a year. And you have to allocate them in optimal quantities at different sites, so that you can deliver a set of finished products at Walmart in Arkansas on Tuesday at 5:00 p.m. (and not 5:00 a.m.) in optimal order quantity, optimal transportation quantity, optimal manufacturing batches, and so on.

Knudstorp learned that many of the LEGO Group's supply chain issues had grown out of the company's commitment to innovation. Allowing product development staff free rein to innovate had led to gross inefficiencies in purchasing, production planning, and distribution.

For example, product innovations involving new colors that were only slightly different from the old colors added a great deal of cost but no real value. In general, designers had not considered the cost of materials in their designs. As they introduced new products requiring different materials, the designers formed relationships with new suppliers. By 2004 the LEGO Group was ordering specialized materials in small quantities from more than 11,000 different suppliers, nearly twice as many suppliers as Boeing used to build airplanes.[9]

The problems resulting from LEGO's undisciplined supply chain and product development processes were not all about cost. Because the LEGO Group had not developed transparency into store demand and inventory levels, the company could not reliably fulfill customer orders. Ultimately, as Lego Group Vice President of Corporate Finance Henrik Weis Aalbæk explained, the lack of supply chain transparency resulted in lost sales.

> Christmas sales are a big part of our revenue (approximately 50%) and we had, for example, pirate ships in demand in Germany, and we actually had too many in France. But we weren't able to see that! And those big boxes, they don't sell very well the following nine months!

LEGO's Operational Backbone Delivers Operational Excellence

To implement the business changes needed to fix the supply chain, Knudstorp deputized an operational team of logistics, sales, IT, and manufacturing managers that met regularly for a year to revamp operations. This team identified 13 interdependent processes that made up their global supply chain (e.g., order to cash, procure to pay, manufacturing, quality). Building on an installed SAP technology base, the LEGO Group then implemented process changes that simplified distribution, cut down on suppliers, and reduced the number of logistics providers. The company also established close collaboration with their largest retailers to conduct joint forecasting, inventory management, and product customization.[10]

Most of the processes in the supply chain business area also needed to be integrated into one or more of the LEGO Group's other functional business areas: Corporate Finance; Corporate Center; Markets and Products; and Community, Education, and Direct. To ensure standardization and integration of the processes in these business areas, the company established formal process teams. These process teams, consisting of key users and often an application architect, optimized processes across all five functional business areas.

Fixing supply chain processes unlocked an 11% increase in revenues, and more than doubled LEGO's earnings from 2005 to 2006. But supply chain optimization was just the first step in creating operationally excellent core business processes. In 2008, the company standardized its human resources systems and processes. It then spent two years standardizing manufacturing processes. As a result, in 2008 and 2009, while much of the world was dealing with a global recession, the LEGO Group reported surging profits.

LEGO's operational backbone efforts did not stop there. In 2011 the company tackled product lifecycle management (PLM). PLM influences more than 80% of the business processes at the LEGO Group, and effective PLM is essential to quickly bringing new products to market. The company targeted an increase in its product pipeline from around 200 products in 2010 to between 250 and 300 in 2012.

Implementing new PLM systems and processes supported better master data management in the supply chain. Together, the PLM and improved master data management increased process automation, which improved product output an estimated 50%.[11] More importantly, LEGO's new PLM system exposed the cost and manufacturing implications of a new product early in its lifecycle, which informed decision-making around product innovation.

Each improvement in LEGO's operational backbone exposed additional opportunities, which leaders have relentlessly pursued. Leaders note that the operational excellence the backbone is delivering fosters additional benefits: faster innovation, enhanced customer relationships, and efficient supply chain processes. In addition, LEGO's operational backbone has positioned the company for digital. Its vision, "developing the builders of tomorrow," requires seamless interactions between physical building experiences and online engagement. As it strives for digital success, LEGO hopes to apply the capabilities of SMACIT and other digital technologies to create greater digital support for collaboration among educators and for the millions of LEGO fans who have created online communities and shared YouTube videos.

Building an Operational Backbone Involves a Business Transformation

As the LEGO example indicates, building an operational backbone is a major, long-term organizational commitment. Leaders must first commit to implementing disciplined, common enterprise systems and processes to replace localized point solutions. Then they must also commit to driving business benefits from the data generated by the improved systems and processes. These efforts will transform a company.

This is the essence of *digitization*. It produces an operational backbone that replaces individual heroes with digitized processes. At LEGO, digitization was nearly a 10-year effort. This is not unusual. Although many companies digitize in fewer than 10 years, developing a powerful operational backbone in a big global company has consistently been a multi-year journey.

Campbell Soup, an $8B global food manufacturer, implemented Project Harmony in its North American operations from 2004 to 2008.[12] In 2008, DHL Express mapped an eight-year journey to implement its standardized European operations processes across the globe.[13] Kaiser Permanente implemented its operational backbone from 2004 to 2010.[14] Even the US Securities and Exchange Commission, a government agency with 4,000 employees, invested three years (2009–2012) in digitization.[15] Philips's efforts to develop its Philips Integrated Landscape (operational backbone) succeeded in standardizing its idea-to-market and market-to-order processes by 2011, but it was still implementing global standards for its order-to-cash processes in 2018.[16]

Digitization takes time because the changes are enormous. The bigger and more complex the company, the longer it takes—and the more likely it is to fail. The issues involve all three organizational design elements: people, processes, and technology. Here are some of the many obstacles to successful and swift digitization:

Big vague goals At large complex businesses, leaders often set unrealistic goals for efforts like ERP implementations. Even in highly diverse companies, management might target a broad range of standardized global systems and processes without clarifying anticipated outcomes. For digitization transformations to succeed, goals must be both clear and achievable. People will then need metrics to help them gauge success. Otherwise, they will lose focus.

Leaders often do not give enough attention to the requirements for organizational change. To implement and execute processes that create reliable core transactions and accurate shared data, people must change what they are doing; they must abandon habits. If they continue to do what they've been doing, the outcomes will be the same. Many people find it hard or undesirable to change habits.

Bad data New systems invariably require investments in cleansing the data from old systems and populating new fields. They also demand ongoing conformance to data capture processes. If people can't trust the data, new systems and processes will have little impact and, even if the systems are implemented, behaviors won't change and benefits won't accrue.

Resistance to enterprise standards Business unit managers must adopt systems and processes that may be optimal for the enterprise but are sometimes suboptimal for their units. As a result, they may lack the motivation to ensure success. If they can get away with it, they may go rogue and just continue to implement the systems and processes they want.

Messy legacy systems Building a foundation for operational requirements requires disentangling a patchwork of messy legacy systems. Although technology is rarely as big a stumbling block as organizational changes, decommissioning legacy applications is not easy, especially when the business needs to continue to run during these "open-heart surgeries."

Misaligned power structures Process leaders must design processes and ensure their implementation across the organization. Often they are not empowered to do so.

Because of these challenges, many companies have initiated digitization transformations but failed to see them through. Companies with high profit margins (e.g., investment banks and pharmaceutical companies) find it particularly hard to persist with digitization, as long as they can afford the high costs of variability in their core processes. Realistically, however, companies without an operational backbone are—or soon will be—at a competitive disadvantage. In fact, while some digital start-ups do not have operational backbones, our observation is that a start-up without an operational backbone is simply in a transitional state. If a start-up does not build an operational backbone, it won't be able to scale. Digital success will be brief.

Although digitization—building an operational backbone—is essential to competing in the digital economy, this book is not about digitization. An earlier book examined digitization in depth, and appendix 1 provides a summary of some of the key points of that book.[17] Although companies have been pursuing digitization since at least the early 2000s, only around 15% of companies have an operational backbone that is widely adopted and valuable.[18]

Shortcuts to an Operational Backbone

To become digital, companies need to overcome the challenges of digitization—and they can't afford to take 10 years to do so. Here are three things leaders can do to accelerate digitization and improve the odds of successfully building an operational backbone:

- Reduce business complexity
- Narrow the scope of digitization
- Lower your standards

Reduce Business Complexity

Business complexity makes development of an operational backbone daunting (and possibly even impossible). Companies that are serious about developing operational backbones can start by identifying non-value-adding business complexity. This may lead to a reduction in the number of products or product lines, clearer customer segmentation, or simpler, more standardized business models.

Like LEGO before 2004, companies can become so mesmerized by innovation that they introduce new products and services without seriously evaluating the added costs of operations, customer service, employee training, and IT support. For example, when Philips embarked on its Accelerate! transformation program, leaders learned that the company had more than 80 different business models. So Philips began its digitization efforts by assigning each of its business units to one of four business models: products, services, software, and systems (i.e., integrated solutions). Each business model had standard business processes. The small number of business models helped simplify Philips. In addition, the company has continued to sell off businesses and eliminate product lines that don't fit its long-term vision. Most recently, it divested its former flagship lighting business so that it could focus on healthcare. As it simplifies the business, the operational backbone becomes easier to maintain.[19]

Unlike many financial services companies, USAA has not developed an addiction to new product innovation. The company has instead selectively added products if and only if leaders are convinced that they are a good fit with existing products and services. Consistent with our research, USAA has observed that product variety does not improve company performance.[20] USAA succeeds in its mission—ensuring the financial security of its members—by focusing innovation on providing integrated solutions rather than increasing product variety. This limits non-value-adding business complexity.

ING Direct Spain is another company that has purposefully avoided non-value-adding product proliferation.[21] As it grew from a mono-line savings account provider to a full-service retail bank, ING Direct Spain introduced a rule that any new product must have the potential of generating at least 5% of the bank's overall revenue. Werner Zippold, former chief operating officer, explained the rationale for limiting product variety:

> You come into a bank and you see this huge fund portfolio of 3,000 funds. And you look at it and say, "Listen, you're basically making 85% of your volume with 100 funds. What do you have the other 2,900 for?" And then you always get the answer: "Well, the clients who buy the Mongolian bond fund are just fantastic. They are five, but they're incredible." So, that's the kind of thing we must not do, because we do not have the margin to support the complexity you get from that.

Our research suggests that business complexity is the enemy of operational excellence. It obstructs development of an operational backbone and, as a result, limits a company's ability to become digital.

Narrow the Scope of Digitization

We have observed that no company has perfect systems and processes. What distinguishes a company with a powerful operational backbone is how that backbone directly supports the company's most critical business requirements. Companies that try to fix everything invariably fix nothing. Many digitization efforts have been thwarted by pointless ambition. Narrow focus leads to faster progress and forces a better understanding of how a company expects to distinguish itself.

One way to narrow focus is to zero in on the one kind of data that is the most important to the business (e.g., customer, product, partner, supply chain) and then devote resources to doing whatever it takes to make that data accurate, accessible, and used. LEGO and Nordstrom both succeeded in their digitization efforts because they recognized the pivotal importance of supply chain data. Focusing on one kind of data limits the scope of a transformation while providing valuable capabilities as a foundation for future digital innovation.

UPS has long benefited from a commitment to protecting the integrity of product data (type of package, pickup and destination locations, date of delivery, sender, etc.).[22] Interestingly, UPS's chief competitor, FedEx, built its capabilities around customer data (name, address, account information, transactions, etc.). You would think that both FedEx and UPS would need both kinds of data. Indeed, they do! But if a company doesn't decide what data will drive the design of its processes, the processes become piecemeal—and all data quality suffers.

These two companies' different decisions about their data had important strategic implications. In the 1990s, FedEx was the higher-priced, more customer intimate of the two; UPS was the disciplined, efficient, lower-cost provider. Over time, each company was able to start mimicking the services offered by the other by building additional processes and capturing more valuable data. They could do so because they had disciplined business processes around their most important data. In short, they had a focused but robust operational backbone.

It's worth having a senior management discussion on this question: If I could have just one kind of master data, what would I choose? Addressing that question forces a discussion of how the company fundamentally plans to operate—a first step toward building an operational backbone.

Lower Your Standards

If you don't have an effective operational backbone and you cannot wait multiple years to build one, there's only one thing left to do: lower your standards! This involves getting help from others to quickly fix what's broken and using off the shelf, "pretty good" solutions. These approaches aren't perfect and you may not want to rely on them forever, but they can get you to "good enough" to start working on becoming digital.

After its massive acquisition binge, Schneider Electric had a product portfolio that could address its customers' full range of energy management needs. But the acquisitions left the company with more than 150 ERP and 300 CRM systems, all supporting customized processes.[23] As a result, it was difficult to provide the integrated products and services that had been the motivation for the acquisitions. From 2009 to 2012 the company made some progress in standardizing processes and reducing the number of ERPs by introducing global function leaders. However, the company was struggling to make real progress with its operational backbone.

In 2012, Schneider sought out Salesforce to help rapidly create a capability to integrate sales across its many product lines. In 18 months the company had enabled cross-selling, which was a huge, albeit limited, step forward. The company continued to gradually replace non-value-adding ERP systems and processes. When it reached 12 remaining ERPs, leaders recognized that those remaining would be expensive and time-consuming to replace. The company wanted to refocus on delivering digital offerings, so rather than continuing to invest heavily in digitization of core systems, Schneider decided to link its new offerings to each of these 12 ERP systems. This is not what Schneider would most want, but it allows the company to focus attention on developing digital offerings, which has far greater strategic impact than tearing out legacy systems.

Like Schneider's adoption of Salesforce, a growing number of companies are relying on cloud services vendors to provide software and even business processes. Vendor services can greatly simplify implementation of critical, but not distinctive, processes, and they often provide data security that exceeds what a company can provide internally. This allows business leaders to hand off a growing number of non-strategic activities to partners so they can focus on key business decisions.

Ferrovial, the Spanish infrastructure services provider, found that digital technologies were opening up many important new opportunities to deliver customer services. Examples included: putting RFID (radio frequency identification) on trash bins to support more efficient trash collection; using big data and analytics to offer variable tollway pricing; designing IoT and mobile devices that helped customers monitor their facilities.

To seize these rapidly emerging revenue opportunities, Ferrovial leaders recognized they needed reliable, predictable underlying core services. But in 2008, Ferrovial had 10 IT units, each providing distinct local support to different parts of the business. Consolidating the 10 IT units into one was a relatively quick undertaking; consolidating all the systems and developing common processes was a much bigger task.

To accelerate the development of an operational backbone, CIO Federico Florez first engaged technology partners who moved Ferrovial's IT infrastructure and communications services to the cloud. He followed that by working with partners who provided HR administration and purchasing in the cloud; Florez insisted that Ferrovial adapt its internal processes to what the cloud made available rather than allow individual businesses to demand exceptions.

This approach to operational backbone development limited debates and helped focus business leaders on deploying technology to improve customer offerings. Ferrovial was shifting its business focus to digital innovation within two years of initiating its cloud initiative. Within four years Ferrovial had a robust operational backbone.[24]

Getting Your Operational Backbone Right

Our research indicates that, although companies have been engaging in digitization transformations since the late 1990s, the majority of companies do not have an operational backbone that will support their digital transformation. In fact, their legacy systems and processes are likely to be an impediment. This chapter developed the following key points:

- Digitized does not equal digital. SMACIT and other digital technologies can contribute to digitization—applying technology to optimize business processes and operations. The goal of digitization is operational excellence. Digital technologies are essential to becoming digital—innovating to create customer solutions. The goal of becoming digital is profitable digital offerings.

- Digitizing involves building and maintaining an operational backbone (a coherent set of enterprise systems, data, and processes that ensure operational efficiency and quality transaction and master data). The operational excellence that results from digitizing is table stakes for becoming digital. That is why we refer to an operational backbone as a digital building block.
- Building an operational backbone invariably requires unlearning entrenched organizational habits, disrupting existing power structures, and installing disciplined business processes that capture critical master and transaction data. Big, old companies have embarked on long, painful transformations to try to implement a backbone.
- Because it's so difficult to implement an operational backbone, most companies do not have one. They should start now to simplify their business, narrow their focus, and lower their standards if necessary to quickly implement some core operational capabilities.
- An operational backbone is never complete. Business changes, coupled with new technologies, provide constant opportunities to enhance technologies and re-optimize critical business processes. In addition, companies are still learning how to take advantage of the data generated within their operational backbones. As they do so, they will identify needs for more and better data, which will lead to further process improvements.

Is your company's organizational backbone "good enough" to support your digital transformation? If so, are you continuously adopting new digital technologies, as appropriate, to update key systems and processes? If not, what are you going to do about it?

4 Building a Digital Platform

A few years ago, when one of the authors was felled by flu, her nine-year-old neighbor offered up his copy of *The LEGO Movie*, which, he said, always made him feel better when he was sick. It turns out that *The LEGO Movie* wasn't much of a fix for the flu. Surprisingly, however, the movie was useful as a metaphor for companies' digital journeys.

In the movie, a noble construction worker sets out to save the world from a tyrant who intends to glue in place all of LEGO world. Emmet, the construction worker, prevails, of course, because he teams up with other good guys who apply their combined creativity to outsmart the bad guys. Key to their success is their ability to reconfigure LEGO components into whatever machine or weapon they need to conquer each obstacle they meet. The not-so-subtle message of the movie is that, if you want to succeed, you must accumulate lots of components and apply lots of imagination in using them. (We have not confirmed with either the movie producers or the LEGO Group that this was the intended message of the movie.)

Digital companies build, buy, configure, and reconfigure business, data, and technology components to generate and enhance digital offerings—rapidly. In fact, componentization is key to becoming digital. Components enable speed and agility because, like LEGO bricks, they allow people to quickly assemble solutions from parts that already exist. The trick, of course, is keeping track of all the components so you have the one you need when you need it. That's why you need a digital platform.

An Operational Backbone Is Not Enough for Digital Success

In chapter 3, we described how the LEGO Group invested 10 years in building a robust operational backbone to support its core business processes. Although LEGO executives consider the company's operational backbone a strategic business asset, former CEO Jørgen Vig Knudstorp noted that the backbone isn't sufficient to address the opportunities and threats the digital economy poses.[1]

> Where we're not savvy enough is in where software development is going now, like smaller applications, disruptive business models, omni-channel landscapes, e-commerce, web-based services, cloud-based services, and so on. We're not nimble enough there. And we could risk ending up with a legacy platform instead of an advantage platform.

LEGO's operational backbone is an asset, but it is not a digital platform.

The characteristics of a digital platform are quite distinct from those of an operational backbone. In particular, an operational backbone provides a tightly integrated, bulletproof production environment ensuring the reliability and security of business *processes*. In contrast, a digital platform provides easy access to the data, business, and technology components that make up *digital offerings*. An operational backbone contributes to customer satisfaction by providing reliability and transparency. A digital platform, in contrast, delights customers by enabling experimentation, rapid innovation, and continuous feature enhancements of the actual offering. Take, for example, Lyft, the ride service. Initially, Lyft offered people the opportunity to request a ride, get picked up, and pay and tip the driver—all on one app. Each of those customer services is a software component stored on a digital platform. Once Lyft had these basic business components, the company started expanding the app's functionality, offering additional services like fare-splitting, intermediate stops, and carpooling. Lyft can constantly enhance its value proposition by creating new components and reconfiguring its offerings with new features.[2]

A Digital Platform—What It Is

A digital platform is a *repository of business, data, and infrastructure components used to rapidly configure digital offerings.* What's so special about a digital platform? Reusable digital components. As they build a digital platform, companies accumulate a portfolio of components that may be useful in future digital offerings. The components are slices of code that perform a specific task. Examples of tasks a component might perform include retrieving a customer's account balance, specifying directions to a location, calculating the probability of an equipment failure from sensor readings, accumulating a customer order in a shopping cart, confirming a user's identity, or presenting performance results in a dashboard. By placing these components on a digital platform, they become available to individuals developing new offerings. Instead of writing code to address all the functionality requirements of an offering, developers can configure an offering by "calling upon" existing components.

To make components reusable (i.e., to enable developers to call upon a component instead of writing new code), developers API-enable components. API stands for application programming interface. An API allows a component to exchange data with another component. In a well-designed digital platform, each component provides an API (i.e., is API-enabled). APIs hence allow pre-defined, "plug and play" connections between otherwise independent components.

A digital platform consists of three repositories built on a base of cloud technologies, as shown in figure 4.1.

- By definition, digital offerings are information-enriched. Accordingly, at the heart of the digital platform is a repository of **data components.** As companies create digital offerings, they will leverage the operational data on their operational backbone, but they will also purchase and collect data from sensors, smart devices and other web services. They will then build (and probably buy) reusable API-enabled software components each of which has code that stores, manipulates, analyzes, or displays some element of that data.

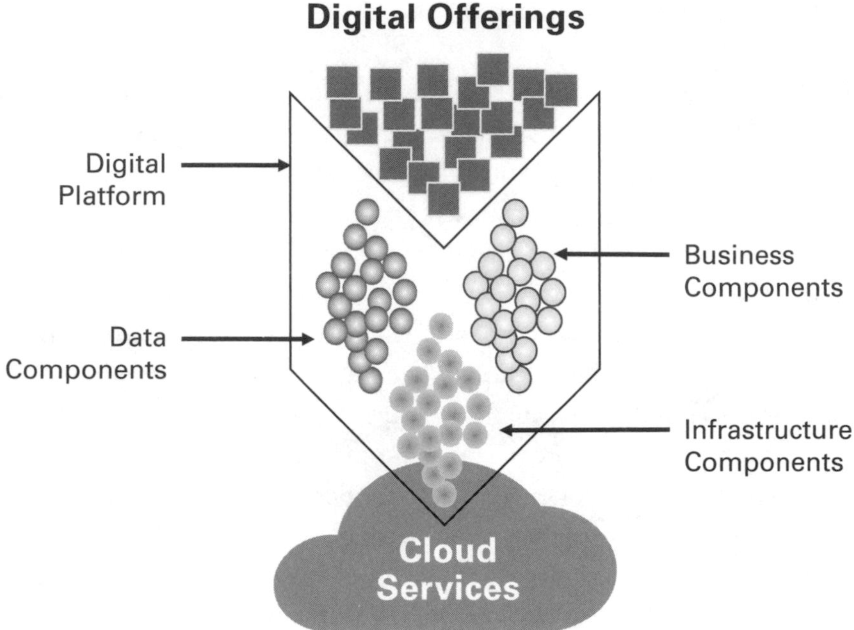

Figure 4.1
Depiction of a digital platform

- A repository of **infrastructure components** provides technical service components to adapt the services embedded in the cloud platform to the specific needs of the company's offerings and customers. These include user authentication and access control, connectivity for smart devices, and orchestration of communication across those devices, as well as services that track usage and ensure data privacy. These components act as a bridge between business components and the cloud services, with the goal of shielding the business components from directly using a specific cloud provider's platform services, and thus avoiding lock-in to any particular provider.
- A repository of **business components** provides functionality required by multiple digital offerings. These services could include dashboards, rules for alerting customers and employees to specific events, onboarding processes that establish new customer relationships, and bots that provide standard support services to customers. Some

companies have more than one repository of common business components because they have multiple unrelated digital businesses.

- The base of the digital platform is a repository of **cloud services** that provide hosting and performance management of applications. These cloud services are fairly standard across vendors. Thus, most companies purchase cloud services from providers such as Microsoft, Amazon, Google, Salesforce, or IBM, but some use private cloud services or a hybrid of private and public cloud services.
- The digital platform services the needs of a company's **digital offerings.** A digital offering is software that includes code unique to that offering (e.g., unique features for a customer segment) as well as API calls to the reusable components needed from the repositories. As the number of digital offerings grows, a company will maintain a catalog of offerings, so that employees, customers, and partners can access them as appropriate.

The digital platform can and should continuously evolve. Toyota Motor North America, which has developed a digital platform to support new car-sharing and other digital offerings, provides an example of how component repositories facilitate development of digital offerings.

Toyota and Servco Pacific Inc.'s Hui as an Example of a Digital Offering Built on a Digital Platform

Toyota Motor North America (TMNA) and Servco Pacific Inc. recently launched a digital offering called Hui—a round-trip, station-based car share service.[3] This digital offering, which is operated by Servco, Toyota's distributor in Hawaii, makes available 70 Toyota and Lexus vehicles at 25 easily accessible locations throughout Honolulu. Honolulu has lots of condos but relatively few parking spots, so car sharing is appealing to both residents and visitors. Hui allows customers to reserve a car by the hour or day through a mobile app that also locks, unlocks, and starts the vehicle.

Hui is one of the first public applications of TMNA's Mobility Services Platform and its consumer-facing mobility services app. Toyota Connected North America (TCNA) built this digital platform for reuse by other Toyota distributors who might want to launch mobility offerings that capitalize on their local expertise.

Zack Hicks, chief executive officer and president of TCNA, and chief digital officer of Toyota Motor North America, heads up development of the digital platform that provides mobility services. He also evangelizes within Toyota the opportunities it creates. He notes that platform development began with recognizing the need for a **repository of data components**. Sensors on cars and phones collect a tremendous amount of data. TCNA considered how that data could contribute to potential functionality for mobility services—providing information on where vehicles are currently located and where they have been; which customers use what services when and how; what kinds of maintenance issues and expenses they have with their various cars, and so on. Technical experts designed processes for capturing, storing, processing and sharing that data.

TCNA also started to create **infrastructure components** built on a **cloud platform**. Infrastructure components allowed TCNA to connect vehicles to the cloud, to authenticate customers who wanted to use services, to link to payment providers, and a raft of other technology services. TCNA also started creating **common business components**, including the mobile app for reservations, the Smart Key Box (which generates a digital key for locking, unlocking, and starting a vehicle via a smartphone), vehicle tracking to ensure availability of vehicles, and payment services.

Hui is one of many **digital offerings** that will use TCNA's digital platform. The value of the platform grows as the portfolio of mobility offerings that reuse components on the platform expands. Soon after launching Hui, Toyota launched a digital offering that tracks buses traveling between two cities in Japan. Because the platform was available, the company was able to roll out this new offering in just six days.

Hicks notes that creating the digital platform did not require a specific understanding of future business models or decisions on the offerings TCNA would create. Rather, he envisioned the importance of mobility services more generally:

> We can stop worrying about which specific business model we are trying to enable by saying, "I need to be able to remotely unlock the vehicle. I need to know who the driver is. I need to be able to score the driver. I need the electronic platform connected to the head unit in a vehicle." These things enable any type of business model, like one-time trunk release for Amazon to do trunk delivery to people's cars at work. That same technology allows somebody to rent a car for

an hour on the streets of Madrid. These are the things that we're beginning to enable that allow for those future business models.

TCNA, the organization charged with designing, building, and promoting Toyota Motor North America's digital platform, was a small team of around 200 people in 2018. Leaders anticipate that customer facing organizations will have primary responsibility for configuring and managing digital offerings while TCNA ensures the repositories for the data, common business components, and infrastructure components. Thus, TCNA will likely grow but it will continue to have an outsized impact for its size.

Digital Platform versus Operational Backbone: Two Different Roles

While Toyota Motor North America relies on its mobility services digital platform to configure new digital offerings, it depends on its operational backbone to ensure the reliability and efficiency of its core business processes. Like most established companies, Toyota finds both benefits and limitations in its existing operational backbone. So, as it builds its digital platform, it continues to try to modernize its operational backbone. For as long as companies require both efficiency and revenue growth, we anticipate they will need to invest in both a digital platform and an operational backbone.

Most digital start-ups focus on a digital platform and are often late to recognize the importance of the operational backbone. In contrast, most established companies have been more focused on building an operational backbone. Some companies, particularly large financial services companies, built legacy systems for each of their products (e.g., mortgages, bank accounts, credit cards). These product platforms are more like monolithic combinations of process and product technology than they are like digital platforms. Unfortunately, moreover, most product platforms in financial services companies were built to support one product. Thus, they do not have reusable components (i.e., APIs). As a result, most financial services companies have many redundant systems and processes supporting their products.

Companies have some options as to what they build into their digital platform and what they build into their operational backbone. For example, customer onboarding can be a reusable business component in a digital platform or an end-to-end process in an operational backbone. Which option makes most sense will depend on whether the company wants to make customer onboarding a customizable experience regularly enhanced through innovation (i.e., a digital component) or a standardized process designed for efficiency and reliability (i.e., a core operational process).

Although some capabilities can be built into either a digital platform or an operational backbone, these two building blocks fulfill different business objectives: efficiency versus revenue growth. Reflecting their very different contributions to digital business success, they also have very different organizational design requirements.

Design Requirements for the Digital Platform

To succeed digitally, companies must define data, business, and infrastructure components and design them for reuse. In other words, they must rethink what they want to offer to their customers in terms of components. The power of a digital platform comes from repositories of reusable business, data, and infrastructure components.

Thus, *the essence of designing a digital platform is deconstructing the company's existing or imagined digital offerings into data, business, and infrastructure components*. This is a very different way of thinking! To help you understand the design requirements for a digital platform, table 4.1 contrasts the requirements for the digital platform and the operational backbone.[4]

As the table shows, the operational backbone and the digital platform differ in five ways: (1) their purpose and outcomes, (2) their technology requirements, (3) their critical data requirements, (4) the development processes that, on the one hand, enable business processes and on the other, enable offerings, and (5) the key roles people take on as they engage in those processes.

Table 4.1
Contrasting Requirements of the Operational Backbone and the Digital Platform

	Operational Backbone (Digitized)	Digital Platform (Digital)
Targeted Outcomes	Process efficiencies, predictability, and reliability leading to increased profitability	Rapid innovation of new digital offerings leading to revenue growth
Technology Requirements	Stable, scalable, secure operational systems; automation of repetitive processes	Repositories of API-enabled business, data, and infrastructure components
Data Requirements	Accurate and accessible transaction and master data	Flexible repositories of big data (from sources like sensors, social media, etc.) for analytics
Process Requirements	Deliberate, methodical design and implementation of transaction-processing applications	Iterative design, development, configuration and commercialization of digital offerings
People Requirements	Process owners and data architects; project leaders for large projects	Platform architects; component owners who can hypothesize, test, and manage functionality of components

Outcomes

As we discussed in chapter 3, the operational backbone supports core business processes. The key outcomes of the operational backbone relate to operational excellence—the table stakes for doing business digitally. In contrast, this chapter has described how the digital platform delivers new sources of revenue, leveraging the capabilities of digital technology to enhance customer engagement and solve customer problems.

Technology Requirements

The key technologies in the operational backbone are those that support increased automation of repetitive processes. The technology should reduce time, cost, and opportunity for error. This involves implementing systems that simplify and increasingly automate transaction and operational processes. These include enterprise resource planning (ERP) systems, customer relationship management (CRM) systems, electronic medical records (EMR) systems, core banking engines, and product life cycle management (PLM) systems. In contrast, the digital platform houses repositories of API-enabled data, infrastructure, and business components, so that the company can quickly configure and commercialize digital products and services.

Interestingly, the operational backbone and digital platform do not differ in the degree to which they exploit new digital technologies. The digital platform exists to enhance digital offerings with new digital technologies like social, mobile, analytics, cloud computing, and IoT (i.e., SMACIT). But these same digital technologies are also playing an important role in the operational backbone.

Although most companies originally built their operational systems on older technologies, like mainframes and on-premise enterprise systems, digital technologies are helping to modernize companies' operational backbones. For example, companies are increasingly supporting core business processes using external, cloud-based software rather than owning their underlying systems. In addition, many companies equip line employees with mobile technologies for easy data access and remote functionality. IoT applications can improve operations, particularly for business needs like equipment maintenance. Enterprise cognitive computing systems apply artificial intelligence to repetitive business processes.

Data Requirements

The operational backbone and the digital platform are linked through data, but they fulfill different data collection and data storage roles. The operational backbone supports the collection, storage, and provision of most transaction and master data. This is because the operational backbone is designed to support business processes that generate and manipulate this kind of data. Ideally, this data will support evidence-based decision-making in firm operations; it will be what some call "a single source of truth."

The digital platform, on the other hand, collects and stores big data—sensor, social media, public, and purchased data—for purposes of analysis and insights about offerings. These distinctions are not pure. For example, some sensor data may be tracking equipment location or functioning in support of the company's internal operations. Moreover, the operational backbone and the digital platform sometimes use one another's data. For example, operational data is often used in analytics embedded in digital offerings, while the digital platform will initiate transactions that then generate part of the company's master and transaction data.

Process Requirements

To become operationally excellent, companies must implement standardized processes where variability would negatively affect the reliability of the company's data or business outcomes. To build their operational backbones, most companies use methodical approaches that nail down as many requirements as possible before any code is written. Even companies adopting software-as-a-service solutions for their operational backbone are deliberate in defining system and process requirements. The processes for making changes to the operational backbone will involve careful planning and testing and periodic releases.

In contrast, the key process requirement for digital relates to the experimentation we described in chapter 2. Digital offerings start as minimum viable products that expand as they demonstrate value. Continuous improvement of components depends on continuous release of software so that customers quickly benefit from innovations and improvements. The number of components in the digital platform can and will multiply. Change processes will be no different from development processes.

People Requirements

To design an effective operational backbone, architects define an "end state" or "target state" specifying the company's core processes (e.g., order-to-cash, global supply chain, HR processes) and how they will share data. Companies can then create roadmaps showing how senior project managers can eventually deliver the target state. These project managers lead large enterprise projects to a timely conclusion. They negotiate, as necessary, for enterprise solutions that are locally acceptable, and they roll solutions out so that value is created quickly.

Architects also play an important role in the digital platform: most significantly, they decide which components are likely to be reused and thus should be designed for reuse and stored in a repository. They may also design standards for API interfaces. But they are not designing an end state. The digital platform constantly evolves as new components are created. Component owners, which we will describe in chapter 5, repeatedly hypothesize and test the value of their components.

The Operational Backbone and Digital Platform Work Together

While the operational backbone and the digital platform are distinct, they must be able to exchange data seamlessly. The digital platform often needs access to master and transaction data both for analytics and for purposes of serving customers. The digital platform might also call upon the operational backbone to provide transaction processing and other functional support for digital offerings. Meanwhile, the operational backbone depends on the digital platform to shield it from constant changes in digital offerings. Figure 4.2 depicts the relationship between the operational backbone and the digital platform.

Because the design requirements of the operational backbone and the digital platform (digitized vs. digital) are so different, companies will

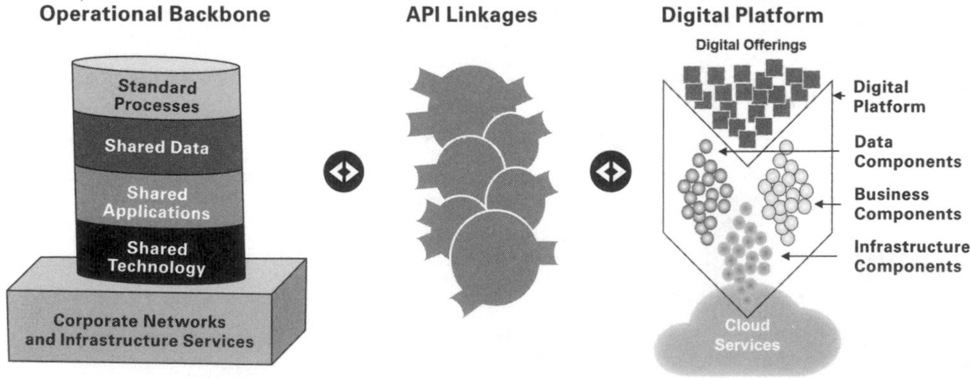

Figure 4.2
Operational backbone and digital platform are linked

benefit from distinguishing the two platforms and the people responsible for each. But the responsibility for creating and maintaining the linkages between the digital platform and the operational backbone belongs to the people and processes associated with the operational backbone. Selecting the right data or the appropriate process to expose to the digital platform requires a sophisticated understanding of how legacy applications and the processes they enable actually work. Extracting and exposing data or functionality similarly requires the use of the careful, deliberate planning and testing processes that are routine for those supporting the operational backbone.

Building a Digital Platform

Our research has found that big, established companies are still in the early stages of building their digital platforms, but that is rapidly changing. In 2016, only 30% of the big global companies we surveyed were building a repository of business and infrastructure components for digital offerings.[5] The remaining 70% of companies had not yet started to design any platform other than an operational backbone. By 2018, however, 74% of big global companies in our research were at least working on building a digital platform.[6] Most of those digital platforms are very early in development, but as business and technology leaders start developing digital offerings, they are finding that a digital platform is essential to rapid innovation.

> Companies with a digital platform are 3 times as innovative (measured as revenues from new offerings) than companies without a digital platform. In 2018 fewer than 5% of companies reported having a widely adopted and valuable digital platform.[7]

A digital platform should be easier to construct than an operational backbone, partly because a digital platform can be built incrementally, as the need for a component becomes apparent. Because most companies have not yet built a portfolio of digital offerings, they haven't (yet) created monolithic systems instead of digital platforms. Be careful—it's easy to start building monolithic digital offerings to address immediate opportunities without recognizing how those monoliths will limit speed when developing future innovations.

The design and development of a digital platform requires thoughtful adherence to architectural principles like modularity, reusability, roadmapping, and standard API design. It requires that business and technology leaders think about the company's digital business in terms of components. We have observed two approaches that can help companies develop digital platforms capable of supporting their business models as they transform from twentieth-century to twenty-first-century companies: building a digital platform incrementally or buying one.

Building a Digital Platform Incrementally

As noted, digital platforms can be developed incrementally—one component at a time. And components can be discarded when they become useless. The digital platform can and should continuously evolve.

Conceivably, a digital platform could start with the components needed for a single digital offering. A successful experiment might expose an opportunity and a company can start to build the necessary components. That approach would delay the launch of these initial offerings, however, so digital companies will be tempted to simply code the functionality for any given offering in a one-off, monolithic fashion. This may work for a few early offerings, but it will lead to rework when a company sees growing opportunities to adapt offerings to customer demands.

Toyota Connected North America built mobility services before soliciting experiments for digital offerings. Similarly, when Hervé Coureil (now Schneider's chief digital officer), was Schneider Electric's chief information officer, he recognized that the company's vision for intelligent energy management solutions would require capabilities that didn't exist in the company.[8] His team built out—sometimes working with vendor partners—four major sets of components that would support future offerings:

1. subscription billing services needed by business models built on recurring revenue from the sale of on-demand services;
2. a set of identity services that associate customers with their products, and in doing so, provide a complete picture of a customer's connected devices;
3. complex event processing that automatically reroutes data from sensors to appropriate operational support systems; and
4. cybersecurity services to ensure the security of data that belongs to their customers.

These components are critical elements of the company's EcoStruxure digital platform. Subscription billing services reside in what we refer to as the business components repository, the identity services leverage data components, and the other two sets of services are combinations of data and infrastructure components. Digital platforms like EcoStruxure position a company for rapid development of digital offerings. But this kind of proactive digital platform development requires a clear vision and an upfront investment that leaders in some companies may be reluctant to make.

The challenge of an incremental approach to establishing a digital platform is that the platform may not seem important (or even worth the trouble) until there are enough components to require formalized management. By the time people throughout a company recognize the need for a digital platform, they may have built a rather messy legacy of monolithic digital offerings for which no one wants to be responsible.

Particularly in companies that have long had autonomous or semi-autonomous business units, business leaders may be unenthusiastic about building and using a digital platform. They would prefer to develop offerings the same way they traditionally developed individual products and services. It's unnatural to think in terms of configuring business components into offerings. As Jeroen Tas, EVP and chief innovation and strategy officer at Royal Philips, notes:[9]

> If you need new functionality, it's always easier to tweak the legacy a little bit. That's why people have a hard time moving over to platforms. Because

> it's always, "I need this little piece of functionality. Oh, let me code it into the existing code base. It's too much risk, too much effort to go to the other platforms." So therefore, as you see in every company, if you don't do something, legacy always wins.

At Schneider Electric, digital leaders had to sell business leaders on the benefits of shared components. Even as they start to get successful reuse, they continue to evangelize these benefits to encourage greater reuse by business units and to stimulate additional development of digital offerings. It is often easier for business leaders to imagine a new offering in isolation than to imagine how existing capabilities might contribute to it. Thus, companies may need to provide incentives or requirements that ensure development and use of a digital platform. In other words, digital leaders often must foster component thinking.

> Companies with a well-developed digital platform, on average, build 61% of their digital offerings from re-usable components compared to 32% for companies with less developed digital platforms.[10]

To help in this regard, several companies we researched had established an architectural role—and a related process—for reviewing proposed offerings to identify components that are candidates for reuse. At BNY Mellon, for example, an individual who is a CIO report is charged with reviewing proposed new or revamped financial services offerings to determine what functionality is most likely reusable by other offerings. She assigns to her team the responsibility for developing the reusable functionality into shared components. Functional leaders remain responsible for developing the rest of the offering.[11] Note that her role, in effect, helps the company think in terms of components.

Designing and building a digital platform requires leaders to recognize and invest in their longer-term needs before those needs are actually apparent. If business leaders don't think in terms of reusable components and then commit to building a digital platform, they risk waking up someday to a set of expensive and fragile digital offerings.

They would be wise to consider the lessons they learned from the messy legacy systems they built in the past. The operational backbone is a challenge today primarily because most companies built systems to meet immediate local needs rather than longer-term enterprise needs.

Buying a Digital Platform

For companies that don't have a digital platform, one option is to buy a start-up with a platform. Such an acquisition can introduce some new digital customer services and accelerate the adoption of digital business capabilities. Northwestern Mutual Life Insurance Company[12] accelerated its business transformation with what Gartner calls a "techquisition"—the acquisition of a tech company to accelerate the development of digital capabilities.[13]

Northwestern Mutual Buys LearnVest

Northwestern Mutual, which was founded in 1857, provides 4.4 million clients with life, disability, and long-term care insurance; annuities; investment products; and a wide range of financial planning, brokerage, and advisory services. Northwestern Mutual is designed as a B2B2C business, providing services to its highly satisfied customers (its renewal ratio is 98%) through a network of financial advisors that has long been one of its competitive advantages. Many customers continue to value their relationship with their financial advisor, and the company assumes that will always be true.

Because its financial advisors have always been pivotal to the company's business model, Northwestern Mutual has focused its systems and processes on meeting their needs. Nonetheless, Northwestern Mutual's leaders recognize that growing numbers of potential customers, especially younger customers with less complex financial needs, are more likely to seek financial advice through digital channels than financial advisors. Many are more comfortable entering data into digital tools than sharing personal information with a financial advisor. They also have little patience for attending a series of meetings. They expect immediate feedback on their options and rapid closure on their financial security decisions. In addition, even customers who value their relationship with a financial advisor increasingly demand online, real-time, and mobile capabilities.

Northwestern Mutual's leaders believe that combining speed, convenience and a delightful customer experience with world-class advisors and products will create a unique winning formula in the industry. Thus, its digital vision calls for offering a portfolio of personal and digital interactions meeting the financial needs of clients with an experience that is dictated by the client.

Feeling an urgency to deliver on that vision, in 2015 the company purchased LearnVest, a born-digital company focused on digital delivery of financial planning for Millennials. The LearnVest acquisition not only provided digital financial planning tools, it accelerated adoption of Agile at scale and other cultural changes. As a result, Northwestern Mutual has been able to accelerate development of both a delightful digital customer experience and new digital tools for financial advisors.

LearnVest, which has been fully integrated into Northwestern Mutual (including its HR, finance, facilities, and technology), has evolved into a set of integrated teams focused on delivering a world-class customer experience. The integrated teams are building financial planning, analytics, and online advice services. The organization, which had 150 people at the time of acquisition, had grown to a 500-person organization by mid-2018.

Buying a born-digital company with an existing digital platform may be an easy, quick option for adding digital capabilities to a company undergoing a digital transformation. But we would like to offer a word of warning regarding acquiring a digital platform by buying a born-digital company. To better understand how digital platforms are built, maintained, and used, we studied the platforms of several born-digital companies: We learned that some of those companies have popular offerings, but they don't always have a well-architected digital platform. They are introducing new features and sometimes even new offerings through brute force (i.e., humans finding a way). They have not carefully designed reusable business, data, and infrastructure components. Instead of components, they have monolithic offerings.

When the leaders of these successful start-ups recognize that their monolithic offerings won't easily scale, they may become anxious to sell their business. Those businesses, however, are unlikely to be a good buy. If the start-up built one or more products rather than componentized offerings, an established company might acquire a digital brand name, but the acquisition will not provide a digital platform.

Companies looking to buy a digital platform through acquisition should also remember that companies adopt different habits as they build a digital platform than they do when they are building an operational backbone. It won't be enough to just acquire another company's digital platform; the acquisition must bring onboard the people and their ways of working. To have an impact on the mothership, anyone engaged in building and configuring components must abandon old habits and adopt those of the start-up.

Getting Your Digital Platform Right

Currently, most companies with established, non-digital business models are allocating most of their resources to digitization—getting better at what they already do. Since they will likely rely on traditional sources of revenue for the foreseeable future and their digital businesses will depend on efficient core business processes, the investment in the operational backbone is wise.

But long-term success is dependent on digital business capabilities, so companies should allocate resources to learning how to componentize offerings and build a digital platform. In most industries, the pace of the shift from traditional products and services to digital offerings allows time for learning how to adopt new systems and processes that will accelerate development of digital offerings. That said, building and using a digital platform requires a very different organization, so companies need to get started on their digital platform building block. If they wait until they have an urgent need for digital offerings, it will be too late.

This chapter developed the following key points:

- Componentization of digital offerings is what's so different about digital. To build a digital platform that can support rapid innovation of digital offerings, you need to think of your business in terms of components. *Do you have any digital offerings that are not componentized? Can you decompose those offerings into components that can be reused in future offerings?*

- Your operational backbone and your digital platform have very different design requirements. *Are you architecting a digital platform with repositories of digital components?*
- The digital platform is distinct from, but works with, the operational backbone. Individuals responsible for the operational backbone will need to make data and processes accessible to your digital offerings. *Do you have people responsible for linking the operational backbone and the digital platform?*

As companies develop digital components and offerings, they become software companies. Software offerings change much more quickly than traditional products and services. Thus, a company's ability to adopt rapid change is key to digital success. Rapid change will demand new decision-making accountabilities and work design. That's what we'll talk about in the next chapter.

5 Building an Accountability Framework

In the 2012 movie *The Avengers,* we see individual superheroes strutting their stuff and winning small victories. When it comes to saving the world, however, it becomes necessary for the superheroes to align their individual talents and work as a team to achieve a common goal. To pull this off, they don't look to a manager to tell each of them what to do. In fact, the film's World Security Council doesn't trust the team and wants to send a nuclear bomb to stop the enemy. The superheroes make a different decision—a better decision—and by both exploiting and coordinating their individual talents, they save the world.

As companies populate their digital platforms and configure their digital offerings, they will be deploying their own teams of superheroes. Individually, these superheroes (which may be teams or individuals in the corporate world) can achieve great things like writing a cool app or developing an artificial intelligence algorithm. In other words, each superhero can successfully create components. But to meet big enterprise goals, superheroes must ensure that their individual components combine to deliver truly remarkable digital offerings.

Traditionally, companies have expected managers to know how to achieve business objectives and to instruct others as to what they should do. That approach can generate business efficiencies, especially when addressing well-understood problems. It does not foster innovativeness.

If businesses hope to succeed digitally—if they expect to develop valuable digital offerings at scale—they will need to empower their people to imagine and build great components. Just as important, they will need to align the efforts of those empowered people so those components work effectively together. This goal of empowering people while coordinating their individual efforts is why companies need an accountability framework. Your digital platform is the technology base for digital success. Your accountability framework defines roles and processes for building and using the digital platform.

Creativity, Not Chaos

Established companies designed for efficiency have usually relied heavily on hierarchical structures. They have done so because command and control management approaches have helped companies implement optimized enterprise processes. When reliability and predictability are the most important characteristics of a process, management will want to prescribe how employees should execute that process.

Developing digital offerings (and their underlying components) depends less on standardized processes and more on rapid innovation. Leaders count on people to imagine what's possible and make it happen. To stimulate creative thinking and exploration, digital leaders are eschewing prescribed, hierarchical processes in favor of empowering people to identify, create, and manage digital offerings. Much like start-ups.

Empowerment pushes decision making to the lowest viable organizational level. Doing so ensures that the people making decisions actually witness the impacts of their decisions. Rather than wait for higher-level analysis, deliberation, and consensus building, decision makers can respond immediately when a change has a deleterious effect on a customer or another employee. These decision makers are also better positioned to think outside the box—to do whatever it takes to solve a problem rather than fall back on normal business rules or processes.

Of course, empowering teams individually to manage digital offerings could easily lead to organizational chaos. Employees responsible for any given component or offering could take actions that optimize that component or offering but fail to further company goals. Companies avoid chaos by developing an accountability framework, which we define as *distribution of responsibilities for digital offerings and components that balances autonomy and alignment.* The accountability framework building block establishes ownership for each digital component.

Most executives recognize that adopting the accountability framework necessary to build and leverage a digital platform (as opposed to an operational backbone) entails making fundamental behavioral changes. Some executives have suggested that they can enact this behavioral change by simply changing incentives. We wish! Incentives are merely one piece of the puzzle in the leadership of a more empowered, more componentized working environment.

Empowered teams establish metrics, define processes, assess outcomes, and adjust their own activities to meet team goals that contribute to larger company-wide goals. To ensure that the efforts of individual teams complement (rather than conflict with) the efforts of other teams, companies must carefully design accountabilities. Clear goals, access to supporting tools and resources, and lots of training and coaching are essential. Otherwise, empowered teams will unleash chaos rather than creativity. You will have components, but you are unlikely to produce competitive digital offerings.

Managing Living Assets

Digital offerings are software based. Because software is intangible, it is endlessly adaptable. Valuable software components can and should change regularly to reflect new learning about what customers want and what technologies can do. Apple, Microsoft, Salesforce, and any other vendor that creates software that people use to perform daily activities have made constant software updates part of our lives. Becoming a digital business will shift your company from one that grumbles when tech partners impose software updates to one that strives to regularly churn out value-adding software updates that benefit your customers.

Because software can and should change regularly, we think of digital offerings and their key software components as *living assets.* They start small and simple and then grow as they attract customer interest.

Eventually, they may be retired. To adapt to customer needs and new technology capabilities, living assets need attention—in many cases, constant attention.

Updates to components are thus an essential part of most digital value propositions, but they place new demands on how people work. People must respond rapidly to new customer insights, which creates a dynamic working environment. It is this dynamic environment that makes empowerment—and accountability—so essential. Hierarchical decision-making processes are too slow, and leaders at the top of the hierarchy cannot possibly be aware of everything that is needed to respond to constantly changing customer demands.

The key role in an accountability framework is that of component owner. A component owner is a team or an individual who is not only responsible for building a valuable component but also for sustaining component quality, cost effectiveness, and usefulness to those who rely on it (employees, customers, and/or partners) throughout the life of the component.

Some component owners are responsible for digital offerings. They develop and maintain the code defining the offering. That code accesses reusable components, as needed, while also providing unique (non-reusable) functionality. Other component owners are responsible for the business, data, or infrastructure components that digital offerings rely on. They make it possible for owners of digital offerings to release new features as soon as they are ready.

It is important to note that creating an organization that can manage living assets is a much more fundamental organizational change than simply adopting Agile methodologies. Agile methodologies change how companies develop software. Rather than invest time upfront developing a detailed set of system requirements, developers surface requirements from users by eliciting feedback on software developed iteratively in short "sprints." To manage living assets companies must assign accountabilities for constantly evolving software components.

Suresh Kumar, former CIO at BNY Mellon, described a component owner as a mini-CEO with total responsibility for the success of his or her product. (No wonder digital management is so hard—digital companies have many CEOs!) A component owner (a mini-CEO) manages one or more components and the value those components generate. The concept is simple, but the implementation is not. Kumar noted that only about one third of his original component owners took naturally to being a mini-CEO. Many, but not all, of the others could be trained.[1] Delivering a great offering or component is challenging. Coordinating individual components and offerings to meet corporate business objectives is an even bigger challenge.

An Accountability Framework Promotes Both Autonomy and Alignment

The biggest challenge companies will face when trying to build and use a value-adding digital platform will not be technical. Building an API-enabled technology, data, or infrastructure component is reasonably straightforward for a trained engineer. It is much harder to define what reusable components are needed, how they will work together, what kinds of enhancements will add value, and what digital offerings have the greatest promise to contribute to business success. That's why companies need an accountability framework. The essence of designing the accountability framework building block is adopting roles and processes that provide enough autonomy to unleash creativity while facilitating alignment across autonomous teams and individuals.

Based on research at companies like Spotify, DBS Bank, CarMax, Northwestern Mutual, BNY Mellon, and others, we have identified eight guiding principles for balancing autonomy and alignment (see figure 5.1 for a summary).

Component owners, not project managers Owners of digital offerings and components retain responsibility for what they create throughout a component's lifecycle. They will not, as project managers do, hand code off to quality assurance, operations, commercialization teams,

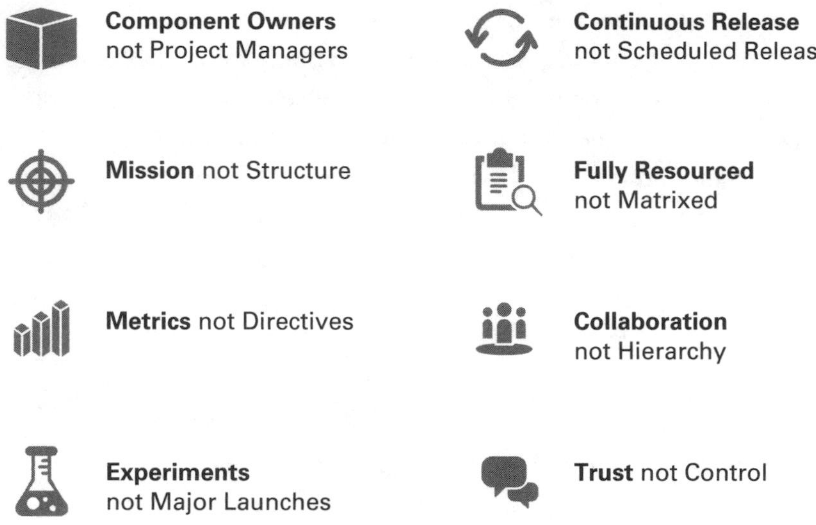

Figure 5.1
Management principles for designing digital accountabilities

or customer service units. The philosophy is "you made it, you own it." The range of responsibilities involved in component ownership is broad and the requisite skills are hard to master. Component owners must be problem solvers; they can't wait for instructions. Many may need coaching to help them learn how to be effective in the ownership role, especially if they are former project managers.

Mission, not structure Formal hierarchical structures provide stability and are useful for reinforcing standardized business processes. Component owners, however, are responding to changing customer demands and new business opportunities. They have less need for formal structures and more need for inspiration. To ensure their activities contribute to company goals, component teams need a specific mission linked to company goals. The mission clarifies what *my team* will accomplish and what *other teams* will accomplish. In this way, a mission gives a team both a goal and boundaries, thus reducing the need to delineate organizational boundaries in formal structures. The mission facilitates autonomy. Teams pursue goals within the boundaries of their mission and coordinate with other teams only when necessary. To sustain the independence of teams, leaders will need to work with component owners to constantly clarify team missions in ways that, as much as possible, avoid interdependencies.

Metrics, not directives To deliver on their missions, component teams need to establish metrics that tell them whether they are making progress on their mission, as they build and enhance their components. To help them, leaders review teams' proposed metrics and debate the suitability of these choices; they do not issue directives. In this way, leaders make optimal use of a team's creative talents and help team members learn what does and does not work. If necessary, leaders will coach a team on how to get better at choosing and pursuing their metrics, but they will not usurp the responsibility of the team to define how it will accomplish its mission.

Experiments, not major launches Teams pursue their metrics by hypothesizing what features or actions will yield the desired impacts. They test their hypotheses by setting up experiments. Invariably, that involves writing some code and releasing it to see how customers (or other teams) respond. Teams compare outcomes from their experiments to the metrics they established. If successful, they can set a new goal. If unsuccessful, they change the hypothesis or try a different experiment.

Continuous release, not scheduled releases To ensure that teams learn and react quickly, they need to release new software code as soon as they develop it. Amazon releases code every few seconds.[2] Most companies don't need to match that level of frequency, but teams cannot wait for periodic, scheduled release dates to obtain feedback. Nor can they rely on an operations team that develops a queue and puts components into production at its convenience. To facilitate continuous release, technology organizations are creating DevOps environments, which minimize or eliminate the separation of responsibility for developing software applications from responsibility for putting applications into production and supporting them.[3]

Fully resourced teams, not matrixed functions For component teams to succeed, they need easy access to all the resources required to deliver on their missions. To start with, that means most teams need to be cross-functional. Even cross-functional teams, however, cannot meet all their requirements for unique expertise. The complex matrixed structures that most big companies have developed to provide horizontal functional services across lines of business and geographies are too slow and too standardized to meet the needs of digital teams. Thus, leaders must trust their mini-CEOs to define and creatively address their resource requirements. Sound expensive? It is. Remember the operational backbone is about efficiency; the digital platform is about speed. Expensive does not mean wasteful. Give your mini-CEOs the resources they need and you get teams that are fully accountable for their outcomes and the costs of delivering them. No excuses!

Collaboration, not hierarchy Well-designed team missions limit interdependencies among component teams. But with so much happening simultaneously in digital businesses, there are times when any given team must coordinate with others. When that occurs, hierarchical decision-making processes are a costly bottleneck. Teams need to learn what other teams they depend on and what teams are dependent on their outputs. Then they can work directly with the relevant parties as necessary. Leaders support these efforts by providing collaboration tools and processes such as co-location, visualizations depicting interdependencies, and weekly stand-ups.

Trust, not control When something goes wrong, the natural instinct of leaders in traditionally hierarchical organizations is to step in and fix it. They need to resist that inclination. A component team with a clear mission and clear boundaries, actionable metrics, and access to the needed resources is in a far better position to fix a problem than that team's boss. Leaders in digital companies coach teams to help members understand what went wrong, or how to go about deciding what to do next, but leaders know far less than the team does about a given problem or its solution. Leaders are not head coaches of sports teams (who synchronize individual activities through command and control) but rather process coaches who help individuals hone their skills at taking full responsibility for a component.

These principles highlight the magnitude of the management changes established companies face as they build and use digital platforms. Even at born-digital companies, these principles are hard to implement. Netflix leaders, who are committed to "freedom and responsibility," note that things don't work perfectly.[4] Indeed, companies adopting these principles observe that accountabilities are constantly evolving. As a company addresses one challenge, a new challenge emerges.

Most of the established companies we studied were very early in their efforts to develop an accountability framework. To understand how such a framework evolves, it's useful to understand what Spotify, the digital music service, has learned after wrestling for years with the dual challenge of empowering and coordinating component owners.

How Spotify Balances Autonomy and Alignment

Founded in 2008, Spotify is a music streaming company offering both free and subscription-based services. Like many other born-digital companies, Spotify is designed for speed of innovation, rather than efficiency. Like many start-ups, the company emphasizes growth over profits. The result is that Spotify's digital platform is more developed than its operational backbone. To constantly enhance the digital platform, the company works to ensure that its digital teams address company-wide business goals while optimizing their individual components.[5]

Spotify has not always had a digital platform. Its initial offering, a desktop client providing music services, was a single, monolithic piece of software. This design was viable when the company's product was simple, but as product teams multiplied and the company added features and subsequent offerings, the monolithic structure—like the legacy systems in established companies—increased business risk. In particular, its monolithic offering limited market response, because new code could only be put into production after every team had thoroughly tested its own code and the company had tested all interactions.

Recognizing the risks of monolithic digital offerings, Spotify reverse-engineered its earliest offerings, extracting reusable API-enabled components wherever possible.[6] Technology leaders then continued to apply modular architectural principles in building the company's digital platform.[7] Half of Spotify's 3,000 employees now build out and use the company's digital platform to design, deliver, and sustain digital offerings and components.

Four mechanisms help Spotify balance autonomy and alignment.

Autonomous Squads Own Components

Spotify assigns ownership of digital offerings and key components to tribes and squads. In general, a tribe owns end-to-end responsibility for a digital offering. For example, the Music Player tribe handles the importing of audio from partners, as well as storing, streaming, search, and a variety of related services.[8] The Infrastructure and Operations tribe, which is the largest, provides most of the infrastructure components.

The tribes are broken into squads, each of which owns one or more components supporting a digital offering or an underlying digital component. The Music Player tribe has a squad responsible for search; the Infrastructure tribe has a squad responsible for the AB test environment. Spotify leaders emphasize the need to define boundaries to limit the need for collaboration across squads.

Fundamental to squad autonomy is the premise that the people working on an offering or component are best equipped to make decisions about it. Accordingly, Spotify does not dictate process or technology decisions to squads. Instead, coaches work with squads to help them learn how to make these decisions. Squads set their own goals, choose their own processes and technologies, specify their metrics, conduct experiments, and assess the outcomes of their experiments against their metrics.

Modular Architecture Supports Autonomy

Spotify has designed a modular digital platform, which means the platform is a set of repositories of API-enabled components (as we described in chapter 4). This design supports a "limited blast radius," that is, it minimizes the risk that one squad's new code will take down another squad's component. For example, one squad's experiment might inadvertently take out the album pictures from the music platform, but because of

Spotify's componentized architecture the problem will be limited to the album pictures. The limited blast radius means that a problem with album pictures does not affect other important components, like a user's ability to play music and search.

Modularity allows the company to create a DevOps production environment. The DevOps environment, in turn, allows teams to put new enhancements and features into production as soon as their code is stable. This allows rapid customer feedback, which accelerates learning and facilitates more experimentation.

Missions Come with Guardrails

The central mechanism for ensuring alignment within and across tribes is Spotify's concept of mission. A mission is a statement of the long-term key strategic objective owned by each tribe (and ultimately individual squads). For example, the mission of the Music Player tribe is "providing fast and reliable access to all the world's music." The mission of the Infrastructure tribe is "enabling high product development speed while maintaining a highly available service."

Missions are guided by—and to some extent help establish—the company's "bets." Bets are strategic objectives for the whole company, while missions define tribes' objectives. Metrics then define how squads will contribute to tribe objectives. For example, a bet could be, "We believe we can increase retention or we can reach x users or more artists by [doing this]." Spotify Organizational Coach Anders Ivarsson explained further:

> "Company bets" are what we call our top company priorities. They are the top 10 things, or the top five things we do as a company. We call each of them a bet, because we actually don't know what the outcome will be. ... We start with what are all the data we have around this? What insights are we drawing from this data? Based on those insights what are our beliefs about the world? Based on those beliefs what is the bet that we're making?

Missions and bets are established both through bottom-up and top-down processes at Spotify. Some ideas come from leadership. More often, ideas come from individuals who work on (or use) Spotify components. Those ideas are then articulated as goals to be achieved within a given time and mapped to clearly defined metrics.

When market conditions change or when the company identifies new opportunities, bets and missions also change. Such changes can require that squads and tribes be reformulated. Change is a constant at Spotify.

Shared Knowledge Sustains Alignment

To synchronize daily activities across squads, Spotify has introduced two coordination and knowledge-sharing mechanisms, chapters and guilds. Chapters are organized around a competency like testing, graphical design, or backend development. Every squad member belongs to a chapter. The chapters facilitate learning that leads to more coherent technology decisions across squads. While squads do not have leaders, chapters have heads who function like line managers, in that they are responsible for the development of people in their chapter. This design fosters flexibility because individuals can move to a new squad without changing chapters. This is particularly valuable for enabling the formation of ad hoc, temporary teams to address a specific problem. Unlike component teams, these teams can form and disband as needed.[9]

Guilds bring together people who share similar interests across different tribes and sections of the organization. Guilds stage internal "unconferences" to share the latest discoveries in their domain and to formulate best practices. In this way, guilds help members develop new skills. For example, a blockchain guild would provide a learning forum for all those people interested in blockchain. Anyone can join any guild.

At Spotify, Agile coaches also play an important role in knowledge sharing, particularly around methodology. Because they work with multiple squads in a tribe, they can recommend practices that other squads have implemented. Other formal and informal knowledge sharing mechanisms include post mortems after failures, where squads can learn from each other's failed experiments, and weekly standup meetings, in which everyone shares progress and surfaces issues that are blocking progress.

Leaders at Spotify note that the company is constantly evolving. No set of practices works exactly as planned and every solution exposes a new issue. Thus, the company constantly redesigns itself to address current issues and opportunities. We expect this will be the norm in digital companies.

Figure 5.2 summarizes the key mechanisms in Spotify's accountability framework:

- *fully resourced* **empowered teams** with clear *component ownership* responsibilities;

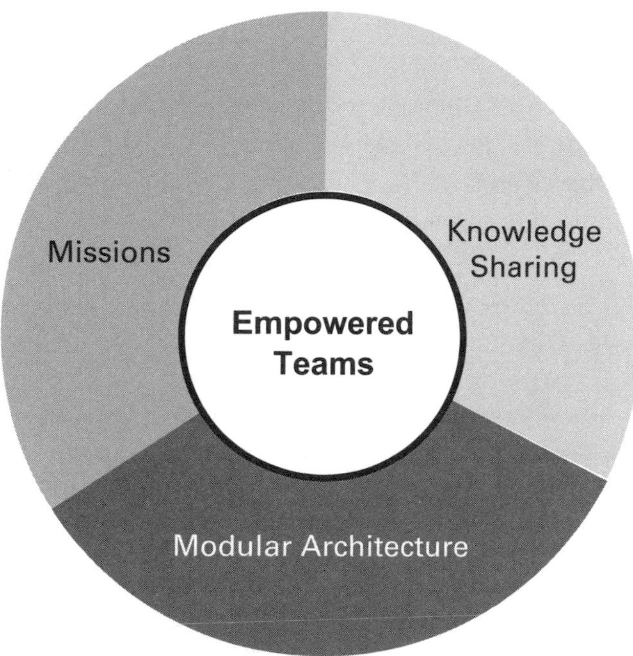

Figure 5.2
Key mechanisms in an accountability framework

- **modular architecture** allowing teams to *continuously release* code so they receive rapid feedback on their *experiments* without risking other squads' components;
- **missions** providing distinct objectives guiding formulation of team *metrics* while supporting enterprise goals; and
- formalized **knowledge sharing** mechanisms facilitating necessary *collaboration*. These mechanisms ensure a balance between autonomy and alignment, so that leaders can *trust* teams to innovate rapidly without creating chaos.

At established companies, the mechanisms supporting autonomy and alignment must complement existing product development and operational processes. Because digital offerings initially generate only a small percentage of company revenues, leaders will want to define an accountability framework that develops digital offerings without disrupting traditional ways of doing business. This means that the mechanisms balancing autonomy and alignment target digital offerings rather than the entire product and service portfolio—at least initially. CarMax, which was founded in 1993 as an online used-car retailer, limited disruption by introducing a new accountability framework only in its digital innovation unit rather than the entire company.

How CarMax Balances Autonomy and Alignment

CarMax, the largest used-car retailer in the US, with nearly 200 stores and 25,000 employees, has redefined accountabilities as part of its efforts to transform the customer experience. CarMax has three lines of business: a consumer business that buys and sells cars, a financing business, and a wholesale car auction business. The company also offers used car buyers various complementary products or services, such as extended warranties, gap insurance, and car financing from other companies. Its new accountability framework includes teams pursuing opportunities to improve both customer-facing and customer-enabling (i.e., associate-facing) experiences. Like Spotify, CarMax relies on the four mechanisms in figure 5.2 to balance autonomy and alignment.

Empowered Teams and Groups

CarMax assigns accountability for building and sustaining components to more than 25 teams of 7 to 9 people with life-cycle responsibility for what they call "products." Product teams are co-located and they are enduring. Examples of products include online financing, search engine optimization, and digital merchandising, as well as platform services. Groups (like Spotify's tribes) of product teams (like Spotify's squads) focus on different stages of the customer journey: Customer Searches, Customer Buys, and Customer Sells. Individuals identify strongly with their teams, even though they formally belong to different functional areas (similar to the chapters at Spotify), most often technology, marketing, or operations. The three key roles on each team are product manager, lead developer, and user experience designer. The individuals in these roles tend to stay together, to facilitate camaraderie and to help teams gel, while other roles are added or subtracted.

Missions

To clarify missions and help both teams and leaders track outcomes, CarMax uses "OKRs" (objectives and key results). As an example, the digital merchandising product team might establish an OKR to grow the click-through rate by 2%. Teams define two-week goals targeting their OKRs. Within a group, the teams share customer outcome OKRs, which align individual product teams with the company's goals for the customer experience. While teams remain relatively stable, OKRs can shift. Like Spotify, CarMax empowers its teams by being specific about the *what*, and leaving it to teams to figure out the *how*. Leaders encourage team members to hypothesize, test and learn. This is a monumental shift from how CarMax operated in the past.

Modular Architecture

To facilitate autonomy, CarMax, like Spotify, uses Agile methodologies to build reusable components for a digital platform. Critical infrastructure allows teams to release code at least every two weeks (consistent with the pacing of their goals). Some product teams are releasing code multiple times a day. As at Spotify, modularity allows teams to change their components without having an impact on other teams' components. This modularity is considered essential to team autonomy and to jointly achieving business outcome goals.

Knowledge Sharing

CarMax applies both formal and informal mechanisms for sharing knowledge to promote alignment across the company's autonomous teams. At the executive level, the chief marketing officer, chief information and technology officer, and chief operating officer talk daily, and they retain personnel development responsibilities for individuals from their functions. Vice presidents in both CarMax Technology (the company's IT group) and Marketing work closely together to provide team coaching. As at Spotify, group leaders shape priorities for their teams and work together to resolve any conflicts among groups—although clear boundaries have limited the number of issues that arise. Teams take responsibility for sharing knowledge in biweekly open houses, where they provide to one another—and to hundreds of others in the company—a 15-minute summary of their goals and results from the prior period. These sessions are live-cast to select CarMax locations and open to everyone. This knowledge sharing provides essential visibility and transparency, which has made it possible for the relatively small number of people on product teams to have a huge impact on how the company does business.

CarMax's accountability framework has facilitated development of new digital offerings. For example, when the company wanted to add an online financing option, a team tested a concept with customers every two weeks and eventually rolled out an offering that allows customers to apply for and evaluate car-financing options at home. An enduring online financing product team now owns and improves the online financing product. This is how digital companies constantly evolve.

How to Develop an Accountability Framework

Many companies are accelerating software development by adopting Agile methodologies. That speed helps companies accumulate shared customer insights through constant feedback and iteration. It can also help populate a digital platform with reusable components—if the teams are charged with that responsibility. But don't congratulate yourself on becoming digital just because you have Agile teams. Agile methodologies alone will not enable your business to create digital offerings at scale. You need an accountability framework that balances autonomy and alignment.

The principles and mechanisms described above can help you design an accountability framework that fosters digital innovation. Be aware, though, that there is no template for your digital organization. You cannot hire a consultant to define a target state. Instead, you will continuously evolve accountabilities to address current needs and resolve problems. Your company will have to *learn* how to succeed as a digital business.

Spotify is constantly tweaking tribes and squads and the mechanisms supporting them. CarMax is transforming through an innovation unit whose empowered teams share their goals and outcomes. Haier, the large Chinese appliance manufacturer, has divided its business into more than 4,000 microenterprises, most with 10–15 employees.[10]

These microenterprises each make market-based decisions about what services to acquire from other parts of Haier and which to acquire on the open market, thus optimizing autonomy. But Haier is also organizing related microenterprises into platforms, which encourages alignment across microenterprises. Every company building a digital platform is learning how to assign accountabilities that will balance autonomy and alignment.

Sometimes that learning will be painful. Leaders that have thrived in hierarchical and bureaucratic environments are likely to be more comfortable telling people what to do than trusting them to innovate and collaborate. They may feel ill equipped to coach rather than direct. Similarly, many people who have settled into a habit of taking orders will be uncomfortable making decisions and taking responsibility for them. In short, developing an accountability framework involves major culture change. Our research has identified some guidelines that help companies adopt an accountability framework and the culture it demands.

- Distinguish responsibility for internal processes from responsibility for new offerings.
- Implement gradually.
- Create coaching roles.
- Rethink governance.

Distinguish Responsibility for Internal Processes from Responsibility for New Digital Customer Offerings

An operational backbone and a digital platform are, as noted previously, both essential to business success, but they play very different roles. In general, the operational backbone enables efficient internal processes and the digital platform underpins innovative digital customer offerings. One measures success in terms of reduced costs and reliability; the other measures success in terms of revenue growth and organizational learning. Companies will be more successful if most of their people accept responsibility for one environment or the other, not both. If individuals throughout the company are constantly trying to reconcile the need for both efficiency and innovation, they are likely to do neither well.

Invariably, teams attempting to develop new digital offerings encounter issues related to the operational backbone. For example, they may not be able to get good customer data; they may need greater visibility into transactions; or they may encounter problems with supply chain processes. The inclination of these digital leaders is to do something to fix what's broken (e.g., build a customer database or overhaul supply chain processes). That is a huge mistake.

Only process owners should fix broken processes. Otherwise, multiple teams will take different approaches to the same problem (e.g., create multiple customer files or fix supply chain processes in different ways). At a minimum, their efforts will be redundant; in the worst-case scenario, they will conflict.

It is useful to distance teams dedicated to supporting internal processes from those that are developing new digital offerings and their platforms. At Royal Philips, for example, the IT unit is responsible for the operational backbone. Responsibility for the company's digital platforms, HSDP and CDP^2, rests with teams under the chief innovation and strategy officer.

Schneider Electric and Toyota Motor North America promoted their CIOs to head their digital businesses and gave them responsibility for both the operational backbone and the digital platform. Their digital organizations, however, have separate leaders for the backbone and digital platform. This arrangement distinguishes individual responsibilities while making it very clear that they are highly interdependent.

Implement Gradually

Autonomy principles allow component owners to address opportunities and issues creatively. Alignment principles ensure that the creative solutions applied to one digital offering complement others and fulfill the company's mission. As a digital platform matures, and the number of employees developing and using the digital platform grows, it becomes increasingly challenging to maintain alignment without curtailing autonomy.

Multiple companies have found that their first digital team can release the first offering with few organizational issues. It's also not difficult organizationally to create a second or third team to support the reusable components of that and subsequent offerings. It doesn't take long, however, before the interdependencies of growing numbers of teams and components create new and unresolved management challenges.

Some companies are transferring large numbers of people at once into agile, empowered organizational environments. If the company has limited experience with defining accountabilities in an empowered environment, this tends not to go well. Start-ups initiate accountability frameworks when they have tens of employees, not thousands. Even then, it is difficult to get this right. Thus, it's better to grow gradually into these new business designs. Remember: if you're trying to act like a start-up, starting small is a design characteristic you'll want to embrace.

A number of companies are learning how to develop accountability frameworks by starting within their IT units. This can be a logical starting point, because many IT people take naturally to principles of componentization and modular architecture. Often they have experience with Agile methodologies. That experience usually results in a preference for cross-functional teams and rapid, iterative delivery.

Northwestern Mutual, for example, sparked its business transformation by realigning its IT people around its three stakeholder groups: clients, advisors, and employees.[11] IT leaders then assigned teams to manage, end-to-end, the digital products associated with each stakeholder group. As part of a commitment to build and enhance living assets, the company has started bringing non-IT business professionals permanently onto teams, and instituting business product owners.

Some companies implement accountabilities gradually by testing out an accountability framework in a separate digital organization. Audi Business Innovation (ABI), AUDI's digital unit exploring new sharing economy–based digital offerings and new ways of working, is a separate legal entity based in Munich rather than Ingolstadt (where AUDI's headquarters is located), which affords its staff significant autonomy. To ensure that ABI helps all of AUDI become more digital, it shares key personnel with AUDI. In addition, AUDI's CIO is a member of the board of ABI, ABI is wholly owned by AUDI, and ABI leaders discuss the business cases for digital offerings jointly with AUDI.[12]

Similarly, in 2016, Toyota Motor North America set up Toyota Connected to isolate digital experiments from ongoing business priorities. Eventually, both AUDI and Toyota hope these digital units will act as nuclei that spread new ways of working to the mothership.

Codifying the principles guiding a company's accountability framework helps make them explicit. Companies like Spotify and Netflix have put their principles of working into writing (and posted them on the internet). Similarly, companies like DBS Bank are finding they need to write down their intentions about how people will work, to clearly establish expectations. Paul Cobban, the chief data and transformation officer at DBS, says he wants to move beyond "typical value words" (think: "team-up," "be decisive," "empower") and provide specific written guidelines on his team's ways of working. For example, instead of just telling people to work across silos, DBS is changing the workspace and increasing co-location to foster working across silos. Cobban is also spelling out what it means to work across silos at DBS. Codifying your culture explicitly helps your current employees discuss it, debate it, and improve it. Externally, it helps to attract the right kind of talent for your company.[13]

Create Coaching Roles

At Toyota Connected North America, an executive leadership team at the 200-person organization defines its role as guiding the group's product (i.e., digital component) owners. The Executive Action Team (known as EAT) meets daily. Zack Hicks, CEO of Toyota Connected North America, describes their efforts as follows:

> Our job isn't to tell them what to do. Our job is to remove the obstacles that are in the way, as senior leaders. The product managers can hire and do as much as they want, as long as they're profitable. So they can reinvest their

> profits. That keeps them focused on what the business wants, and what the customers want. We do give feedback. I do one-on-one sessions with them, but it's not to manage their daily activities.

Spotify emphasizes the role of its Agile coaches in helping teams define their processes and deliver to their missions. Companies are engaging Agile coaches for roles varying from teaching Agile methodologies to offering support for leaders who oversee digital teams.[14] Because leaders will find coaching an increasingly important part of their roles, most will need coaching on how to coach well.

DBS Bank assigns a partner from its transformation office to the leaders of its autonomous teams, to help them learn the new "CEO" aspects of their responsibilities. It refers to the partner as a "Sherpa"—someone to help the team learn how to articulate and achieve its goals. Sherpas provide templates, methodologies, and guidance for the team. The transformation team wants to make sure that people within DBS feel equipped to handle their ever-changing roles. DBS is also heavily investing in formal employee training in innovation, Agile methodologies, evidence-based management, and related skills. This kind of investment is likely essential to changing an organizational culture. It will not serve companies well to design digital offerings but fail to invest in the people who will be key to the long-term success of those offerings.

Rethink Governance

Many leaders think of governance as the decisions that rest with senior executives related to formulating business strategy and aligning resources to ensure execution of that strategy. We have defined governance as specifying who makes—and is held accountable for—what decisions.[15] Building an accountability framework is a governance effort.

The accountability framework for digital devolves many decision rights to autonomous teams while creating a context to help these teams make the right decisions. Paul Cobban explains what DBS is doing to push accountability down:

> You have to set a clear outcome, and give people boundaries—what we call "the electric fence." We are trying very hard to define the values very clearly,

> so people know when they are about to grab the electric fence. Anywhere inside the fence, and as long as you're moving towards your goal, you're empowered to do whatever you want. We're trying very hard to coach people and teach people how to empower their teams.

Traditionally, the most important senior executive governance decisions in a company have involved the allocation of resources. After establishing business strategy, executive leaders would design structures allocating responsibilities for executing that strategy, and then make investment decisions to provide the resources for strategy execution efforts.

In digital organizations, the most important senior executive governance decision relates to the defining of missions. Well-defined missions enable autonomous teams to focus on meeting their goals. Because they are accountable for the costs and benefits they generate, teams are less likely to seek resources they cannot convert into value. If the missions are poorly defined or insufficiently distinct, the efforts of empowered teams will collide and company goals will be at risk. This is why defining clear missions supplants resource allocation as the key governance decision in digital organizations.

Most of the companies we have studied fund experiments knowing that some will fail. Those experiments usually have a short life. Many companies require that an experiment yield a minimum viable product (MVP) in two to three months. Future funding depends on demonstrating value. As one digital business head described the process:

> If we're seeing steady releases, then we'll continue to fund them. If we don't see steady releases, or they are not able to break through with customers, then they're going to have to go through more governance.

Once teams become established, they tend to have a sustaining budget, but leadership teams monitor their results to ensure teams stay on track. Zack Hicks at Toyota Connected notes that because teams are specific about their missions and metrics, everything is visible:

> I understand what's in progress, what was released this week, and what's their burn down chart. This is how, over a period of time, I can see how much they're actually producing.

Senior executives will continue to make key decisions about which new strategic initiatives to pursue and which to forego. This includes investments in infrastructure components like the decisions Toyota, Schneider Electric, and Philips made to invest in connectivity. Some of these decisions may feel like venture capital decisions—identifying business experiments worth testing. Philips's executive team explicitly considers the reusability of an offering (or its underlying components) as part of its decision on what digital offerings to fund.

At successful digital companies, leaders will make it a daily task to identify new offerings worth pursuing and new issues that are obstacles to digital success; leaders will then find people to own the missions related to these new opportunities and challenges. It may take time for people accustomed to fairly stable organizational structures to become comfortable with constantly evolving accountabilities. Over time, however, continuous change in accountabilities should become second nature.

Getting Accountability Right

Our research suggests that established companies are very early in their understanding and application of accountability frameworks that are essential to digital success. But they are learning! Their traditional reliance on organizational structures to allocate responsibilities will surely die hard. But once they adapt to an environment in which they see a problem or opportunity and immediately empower a team or individual to own that mission, they are unlikely to look back. Here are the key lessons from this chapter:

- To build and use a digital platform, some people in your company will have to fundamentally change the way they work. Essentially, your company will have to act more like a software company, and that means assigning ownership for living assets. *Have you adopted Agile methodologies? Do you assign and empower owners for living assets?*
- To avoid chaos, as you empower teams, you need an accountability framework for your digital business that balances the autonomy

of individual teams with alignment across them. This will require identifying distinct missions for your teams. *Have you identified missions for your individual teams that minimize team interdependencies? Is someone taking responsibility for constantly tweaking your accountability framework to respond to organizational learning about what works?*

- Facilitating innovation requires fully resourcing your innovation teams. If your innovation teams have to survive on a shoestring, they will not generate new value propositions or digital offerings. Mini-CEOs can eventually accept responsibility for covering the costs of their components and offerings, but they need start-up resources. *Have you made a financial commitment to generating digital offerings?*
- Because companies have limited experience with the management principles that support empowerment and componentization, companies should start small and allow for organizational learning. *Have you established a few autonomous teams and a process for learning how to make them effective?*
- Managers in digital organizations rely more on coaching than hierarchical decision making to optimize business outcomes. *Are you investing in helping your people to become great coaches?*

Building your accountability framework may be the hardest building block of all. Find the biggest obstacles to your company's ability to manage living assets. Start experimenting to learn how to get your accountabilities right.

6 Building an External Developer Platform

To be a child is to imagine how cool it will be when you're grown up. Then you'll be able to do things like drive a car, hang out at a shopping mall with friends, stay up late at night, kick a football far across the field, wear lipstick, or smoke a cigarette. Clearly, some aspirations are both achievable and desirable. Others prove to be unimportant, even undesirable, or unachievable.

Companies that were not born digital are just starting to imagine what it will be like when they are digital. As they transform, they will achieve some of their aspirations. Others will prove to be unimportant, even undesirable, or unachievable.

Our conversations with executives suggest that many companies in the early stages of digital transformations aspire to power an entire ecosystem—you know, like Apple. The idea is to create a platform like iOS and make its services available to third-party app developers. Those developers then sell their apps to your customers and you tax the revenues. Next thing you know, your market capitalization is skyrocketing.

Of course, this is not the way every company's aspiration will pan out. GE built its Predix platform to collect and analyze IoT data in ways that would improve management of customers' industrial assets.[1] GE anticipated that external developers would create components to expand the functionality of the Predix platform. But customer demand developed slowly and developers didn't demonstrate much interest in providing the expected functionality.[2]

Despite this cautionary tale, most companies will find value in extending their digital platform to support ecosystem partners.[3] What is actually desirable and achievable in these partner relationships is another question.

The Apple Aspiration

It's worth noting that Apple's ecosystem of app developers was not part of the company's initial business model. Early on, Apple's internally developed applications capitalized on the mobility and connectivity capabilities of digital technologies. Before inviting external developers to post apps in the App Store, the company had become internally proficient at creating apps: the browser, the email client, the short messaging services tool, the camera, the weather app, and the productivity tools. Although Steve Jobs initially resisted opening the iOS platform to external developers,[4] he eventually recognized that Apple did not need to own all the apps. By then Apple was in the driver's seat. Because Apple owned the underlying infrastructure and access to customers, app developers could see huge benefits from building their digital offerings on Apple's platform.

Unless you can provide the best solution to your customers' every need all by yourself, you, like Steve Jobs, will *have* to tap into the creativity of outside parties as you generate digital offerings. Otherwise, you'll find yourself, poorly equipped, competing against alliances of powerful companies. Urgency is also a factor. While a company may prefer to develop its own components rather than use partners' components, its customers may have little patience for the time it takes to do that. Thus, ultimately, an ecosystem will be important to most companies' digital success.

The business models of many by now legendary digital start-ups, including Salesforce, eBay, Uber, and Facebook, are based on ecosystems. Indeed, the hype around ecosystems is creating a sense that everyone can and should build a winning platform that links a vibrant community of third-party providers and consumers.

An ecosystem is a business model that seeks to connect multiple sides of a market (e.g., app users and app developers on iOS; drivers and ride-seekers on Uber; posters, readers, advertisers, and game developers on Facebook), so they can interact directly with each other. Ecosystems exhibit virtuous-circle, cross-side network effects: the more participants there are on one side (e.g., developers), the more value will be created for participants on another side (e.g., users) and vice versa.[5]

It's more exciting to focus on the brilliance of this strategy than on the embedded culture that will hinder a company's ability to deliver on it. As earlier chapters have detailed, companies learn how to build and manage platforms of reusable digital components over the course of a long journey. Opening up a company's components to external parties adds another set of design challenges. To address those challenges, you will need a fifth building block: an external developer platform.

An External Developer Platform Extends a Digital Platform

An external developer platform (ExDP) is *a repository of digital components open to external partners*. It's useful to think of two different kinds of external developer platforms:

1. **An ExDP that allows partners to use the company's internally developed components in the partner's offerings.** For example, the Google Maps ExDP makes functionality and data related to Google maps available to external developers for use in other companies' offerings.[6] Kabbage's ExDP makes its automated lending engine available to other financial services companies.[7]
2. **An ExDP that provides an industry platform by creating a market for related digital offerings.** For example, Apple invites application developers to make their offerings available to owners of Apple devices through their App Store. Similarly, Salesforce offers extensions developed by third parties to their customers through their AppExchange.

An ExDP supports ecosystem partnerships by securely exposing digital platform components via APIs to external parties. (Recall that an

API—application programming interface—is the code that allows one component to request another component to complete the task it was programmed to do.) To facilitate partner use of internally developed API-enabled components, external developer platforms usually include a developer portal that provides a catalog and descriptions of all available components (often referred to as APIs, for short). ExDPs also provide tools like software development kits (SDKs) to help external developers quickly write new code that leverages the services performed by the platform's components.[8]

In chapter 4 we described digital platforms as repositories of digital components—data, infrastructure, and business components. A well-designed digital platform consists of API-enabled components. The APIs give a company the ability to configure offerings from components in a modular, "plug and play" fashion rather than writing a monolithic heap of code for each offering. Once an API is developed, its security and governance features dictate who can access the API, and thus use the underlying service. In essence, an *external* developer platform (ExDP) extends to external parties access to the APIs for a selected set of components on a company's digital platform. Companies can offer open access to APIs through a public online developer portal or they can limit access to selected partners. Figure 6.1 depicts the relationship between a company's digital platform and its external developer platform.

Some companies have an urgent need to manage external access to their digital platform. For example, as part of efforts to give individuals greater control over their data, open banking requirements in Europe and Australia require that the largest financial services companies allow verified third parties to access customer account information or initiate payment services via APIs.

Westpac New Zealand, part of Westpac Group, a large financial services company, developed figure 6.2 to describe how it intends to provide access to customer data and related banking services to external parties. The ExDP accesses business and data components residing in the company's digital platform, which, in some cases, will access data and

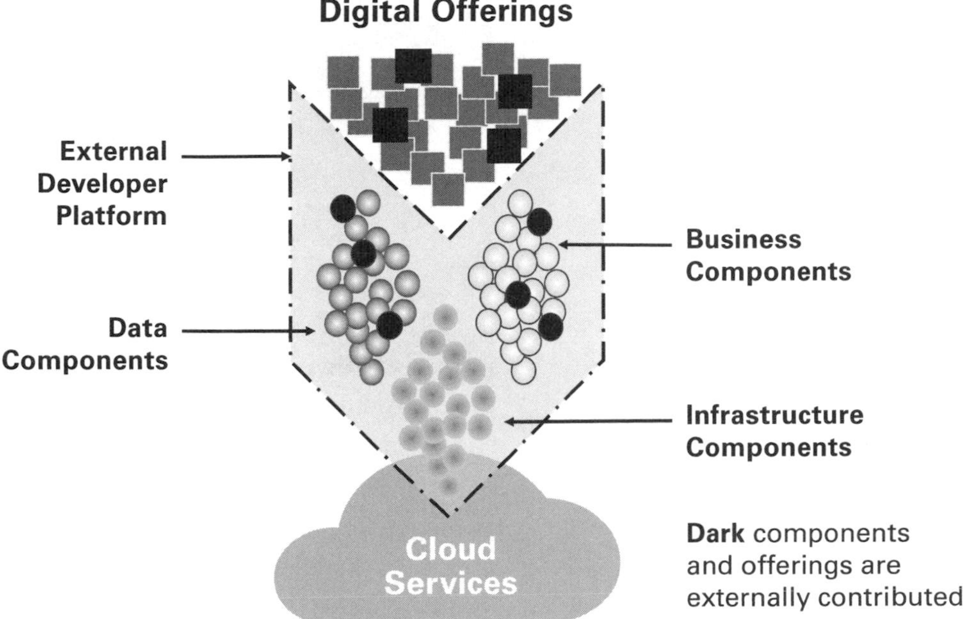

Figure 6.1
Ecosystem enabled by an external developer platform

link to processing in the company's operational backbone. (Another reminder that the operational backbone is table stakes!)

Westpac technology leaders have observed that the ExDP establishes new relationships with third-party developers. These developers are not only partners but they are also, in effect, customers of the company's APIs. As companies create their ExDPs, they will be defining business models for this new kind of customer—one that develops additional services for the company's end customers.

The established companies we researched are in the early stages of building their external developer platforms.[9] Because it's such early days, best practices are just starting to emerge. DBS Bank in Singapore, Uber, Royal Philips, and Schneider Electric provide examples of how companies are approaching external developer platforms. DBS and Uber are providing business and data components that partners use in developing their

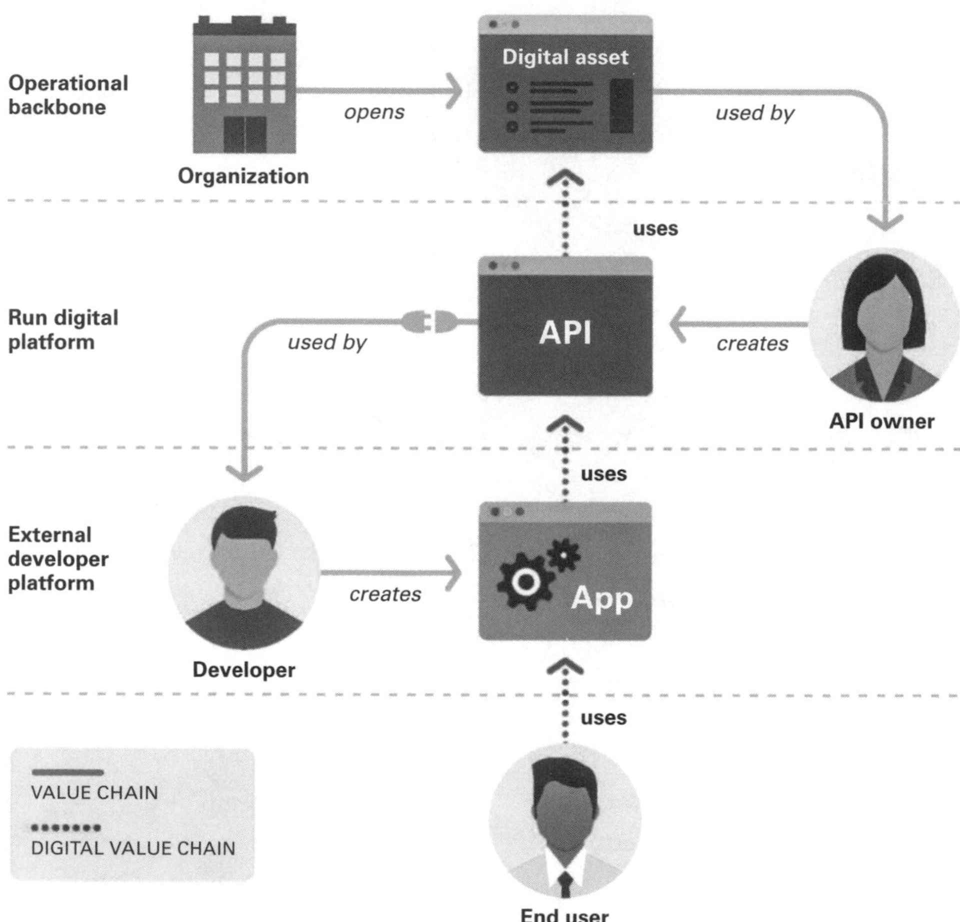

Figure 6.2
Westpac's depiction of how its external developer platform works
Source: Westpac New Zealand Limited

offerings. Philips and Schneider are developing industry platforms that provide the infrastructure for other companies' offerings.

> In 2018, only 1.5% of established companies had a widely adopted and valuable external developer platform. Another 11% of companies were in the process of rolling one out.[10]

DBS Bank Provides Banking Services to Partners

DBS Bank offers its outside partners access to more than 200 API-enabled digital components. Although some components provide infrastructure services (such as an authorization service for secure access to DBS's APIs), most components provide business and data services. These include credit card management, calculation of loan eligibility, a listing of customer channel preferences, calculation of foreign exchange rates, a listing of DBS ATM locations, a wide variety of payment services, and some analytics services such as customer spending patterns. DBS brands some of the products (e.g., DBS credit cards, DBS ATMs); in other cases, the partner's customer might be unaware of DBS's role.

DBS is still learning what kinds of ExDP services and related business models will maximize benefits for customers, third parties, and the bank itself. Some components, like those related to credit cards, could increase DBS's revenue from credit cards. In other cases, DBS is targeting customer satisfaction. The company measures the benefits in terms of "customer stickiness." For the most part, DBS is not attempting to generate revenues on component usage fees at this time.

The value to DBS's partners is their ability to quickly ramp up digital offerings that have a financial (e.g., payments) element. Partners can focus on developing unique digital offerings by taking advantage of DBS's core capabilities rather than try to duplicate them (and compete with DBS on what might become commodity services).

One partnership that is generating benefits for all stakeholders is DBS's partnership with soCash, a fintech[11] that developed an app allowing a user to locate a participating retail store (like a 7-Eleven) and "withdraw" money from the store's cash register by using the app rather than by finding an ATM. In the background, the soCash app is interacting with DBS's external developer platform APIs to withdraw money from the user's account with DBS and deposit it in the merchant's account. DBS does not receive any fees from soCash. Instead, DBS benefits from a decreased need to stock ATMs with cash. DBS also realizes increased satisfaction on the part of its customers who enjoy the convenience of accessing cash when no DBS ATM is nearby.

Another DBS partner, Tally, an Indian ERP software provider, is enabling straight-through processing of payments using DBS's payments API. Business customers using the Tally ERP can initiate the transfer of funds from their DBS account to suppliers, for example, right from their ERP when they execute an accounts payable transaction. This saves a step in a customer's accounts payables processing.[12]

DBS initially experimented with the value of an ExDP by inviting 15 start-ups to a two-day hackathon to see what start-ups might be able to offer based on an initial list of APIs that could possibly be provided on an external developer platform. The start-ups had many viable business ideas. They also identified some additional business APIs that DBS had not considered. Since the hackathon, DBS has been moving aggressively to offer services externally.

To make it easy for partners, DBS provides a website portal where potential partners can view a catalog of its digital services.[13] For new partners who become interested in accessing its digital services, DBS lays out a 3-step process:

1. Sign up on-line for a DBS developer's account.
2. Experiment in a secure sandbox, where the partner can test a linkage to the DBS API.
3. Request production access so that the connection to the DBS service goes live.[14]

Exposing digital components externally has highlighted for DBS the importance of a well-designed and -managed internal digital platform. Initially, DBS allowed individual business units to develop their own API-enabled components. This accelerated innovation within the lines of business but it led to duplication across the lines of business, and essentially resulted in each line of business developing its own digital platform.

When DBS decided to offer components externally, leaders realized that their multiple digital platforms meant that they would be presenting multiple external developer platforms to potential external partners. This would make it harder and less appealing for developers to partner with DBS. Technology leaders have used these concerns about DBS's ExDP to initiate discussions on rationalizing and consolidating relevant internal digital platforms. DBS Innovation Group's Head of Innovation, Bidyut Dumra, explained how they handled this challenge:

> We knew we were not going to be the "first" financial developer portal, so we set our ambition on being the "best." This translated into a vision of having a single public-facing portal for partners and enabled us to bring all the lines of business and system owners to the same table to discuss and decide on how to make it happen. The resulting developer portal was launched in November of 2017 as the

largest financial API portal globally, with over 150 APIs and 50 live partners using its services.

DBS is developing a single catalog of its more than 3,000 internal APIs. This effort will facilitate both internal and external reuse of digital components.

To encourage potential partners to participate in its ecosystem and to scale the use of its ExDP, DBS is investing in a new ecosystem partner engagement process. On the business side, the process includes opportunity discovery and partner onboarding, as well as the definition of joint commercialization and marketing options and the tracking of relevant business metrics. On the technical side, it involves security vetting, the identification of relevant new and reusable APIs, and the definition of how a service will be supported by DBS and the partner. DBS is finding that implementing—and where possible, automating—standard processes for partner management is important to driving value from an ExDP.

DBS expects its external developer platform to leverage its digital offerings and expand the services available to its customers. Uber has been exposing its APIs to customers for a number of years. It is still learning how to capture the opportunities and manage the challenges of an ExDP.

Uber Supports External Developers

Uber, which launched its ExDP in 2014, has a team of more than two-dozen people taking responsibility for oversight of platform development.[15] This team aims to empower developers—particularly external developers—to build what the company refers to as "moving experiences." The APIs exposed on Uber's external developer platform are, in effect, digital offerings for external developers and *their* customers. For Uber, the key benefit of its external developer platform is that external developers create digital functionality that increases demand for Uber services.

Uber has an Affiliate Program to encourage external developers to create apps and applets that drive business to Uber.[16] In turn, affiliates are rewarded US $5 for each new US-based customer they refer to Uber. The company's ExDP provides external developers with access to API-enabled business components, as well as to software development kits. Uber also makes available integration elements (such as buttons and widgets), which enable partners to give their customers access to Uber rides with a simple click of a familiar-looking Uber icon.

Uber provides access to its digital platform through three major sets of APIs: one focused on ride requests and in-ride services; another focused on drivers; and a third on business customers. Through these sets of APIs, Uber offers a variety of functionality with which third parties can create new digital offerings.

For example, Payfare, a financial technology company, built an app leveraging the Uber Driver API. Individual drivers can sign up with Payfare to authorize daily (instead of the usual weekly) payment for the Uber driving they do each day. Payfare captures drivers' earnings data in real-time. Then, for a 1% fee, Payfare processes payments directly to each driver's Payfare Mastercard account. The Uber-Payfare partnership generates benefits for all stakeholders: Payfare benefits from the fees drivers pay; Uber benefits from its ability to better attract and serve drivers; drivers get cash when they need it.

Of course, many potential partnerships fail—a reminder that companies must generate shared customer insights related to their ExDP services. For example, in 2014, Uber created UberRUSH, a delivery and logistics service for small businesses that used Uber drivers to deliver packages and other items. Uber built the UberRUSH API to allow both internal and external developers to add logistics services like real-time tracking, signature confirmation, delivery price quotes, and summary reporting for Uber's business customers. Uber's expectation was that increased logistics functionality would make the company an increasingly desirable transportation option for businesses. In other words, the benefits to Uber would be increased transportation revenues.

UberRUSH attracted mostly small start-up businesses, like an on-demand dry cleaning service, various restaurants, and a peer-to-peer drone marketplace. Apparently, however, UberRUSH consumed resources, specifically drivers, in ways that generated less revenue than standard Uber services for both drivers and the company. As a result, in 2018, Uber shut down UberRUSH (and thus its API).[17] This kind of test-and-learn experience is common as companies start building their ExDPs.

Uber's Developer Platform team includes a developer-relations team, an API platform team, an API features team, and partner software developers.[18]

The team establishes priorities for development of both its digital platform and its ExDP. Team members identify internal needs by working with their business development colleagues. They also get ideas from external developers, through one-on-one interactions and a variety of forums and hackathons held around the world. They target large industry players (e.g., Hyatt, United Airlines, StubHub!, and Amazon Echo), all of whom facilitate Uber ride requests for their customers. Uber also attracts a long tail of developers who build applications for niche markets.

ExDP governance at Uber is mainly focused on generating opportunities. Accordingly, Uber gives business partners full control over data that flows into the partners' applications. Sales and business development teams negotiate contracts and specific terms of use with large brand-name partners. For all other external developers, Uber has established standardized terms of use to which the developer commits when accessing ExDP functionality. Uber closely monitors uses by third parties and the terms of use indicate that Uber can implement a "kill switch" if it perceives a partner is misusing a service.

DBS and Uber are exposing business and data components to third-party developers. Philips and Schneider do some of the same, but their visions are more focused on creating industry platforms by also exposing infrastructure components.

Philips Builds an Industry Platform

Many companies aspire for their ExDP to become an industry platform (like GE's Predix). For example, Philips is building an industry platform for healthcare. Philips's ExDP leverages the company's digital platform, HSDP[19] (HealthSuite Digital Platform), providing access to components that will allow partners to build applications on its core infrastructure.

Whereas DBS and Uber are primarily providing partners with access to business and data components, companies building industry platforms are more likely giving their partners access to infrastructure components. HSDP, for example, provides infrastructure components on an

Amazon Web Services (AWS) cloud foundation. In particular, HSDP has built seven categories of technical components that facilitate access to and control of IoT sensor data generated by healthcare technology and equipment:

- **Authorize**—provide centralized identity and access management and ensure data privacy
- **Host**—provide tools to monitor system status and application performance across global deployments
- **Connect**—manage, update, monitor, and collect data from smart devices ranging from consumer-grade wearables to large medical systems
- **Store**—acquire, access, and manage data from applications through a cloud-hosted repository
- **Analyze**—furnish the infrastructure to build decision-support algorithms and machine-learning applications
- **Orchestrate**—provide tools for workflow optimization, rules management, routine task automation, and communications coordination
- **Share**—provide interoperability between HealthSuite-enabled applications and devices with external third-party systems

Philips has opened its external developer platform to a "by invitation only" group of friendly external developers. This can expand as the company builds a bigger portfolio of components and can better identify the opportunities to leverage the company's ExDP. Over time, Philips expects internal and external applications built on HSDP to facilitate greater individual control over healthcare data and greater integration of data within healthcare systems. If large numbers of healthcare providers and customers rely on HSDP, Philips will likely start generating revenues not only on its digital offerings for healthcare customers but also on its provisioning of a healthcare industry platform.

Although Philips is experimenting with making selected components available (i.e., analytics and AI services) to third parties, the company is concentrating on building up its internal digital platform. That focus should accelerate development and reuse of the company's internally developed components. Philips's growing portfolio of offerings will almost surely provide useful components for third parties, when it's ready to take on that management challenge.

Schneider Electric Creates an Ecosystem for Energy Management Solutions

Like Philips, Schneider Electric envisions offering an industry platform. Schneider recognizes that its industry is facing a major shift in its approach to innovation. This shift is revolutionizing the customer experience and engagement. It is also re-centering the conversation between suppliers and buyers around solving problems instead of building better equipment. Accordingly, Schneider has developed Schneider Electric Exchange,[20] an ExDP designed to support an ecosystem of IoT energy management and automation solutions suppliers and buyers. The ExDP allows ecosystem stakeholders such as developers, data scientists, end-users, inventors, entrepreneurs, and more to create, collaborate, and scale solutions. Schneider, through its ExDP, orchestrates this open ecosystem.

To interest external developers, Schneider Electric kick-started its ExDP in April 2018 by identifying several challenges that needed to be addressed. A hackathon invited external developers to propose solutions to three challenges. The best solutions received a reward. To prepare for the hackathon, Schneider identified APIs to share analytics and data sets that would be most important to developers trying to address the proposed challenges. In this way, Schneider Electric is both building its ExDP (Schneider Electric Exchange) and gaining offerings developed by third parties. The company plans to conduct additional hackathons as it develops and exposes developer APIs. By increasing digital offerings available on its exchange, Schneider generates more traffic and positions itself as an ecosystem driver.[21]

Industry platforms, like those Philips and Schneider are developing, have the potential to generate revenues from taxes on partners who use the platform to sell digital offerings. For any company developing such a platform, however, future revenue streams are not assured. Companies have to experiment to learn how to create a revenue-generating ExDP value proposition.

Who Needs an External Developer Platform?

A company's external developer platform allows it to expand the number and scope of customer offerings and generate new revenues or increase customer satisfaction. In short, an external developer platform allows a company to reap advantages of scale. Because the distribution costs of software are immaterial, reusing digital components offers a theoretical opportunity to increase their value at near-zero cost. In other words, an ExDP increases the payback on investments already made in a company's digital platform.

This does not mean that an ExDP is "free." Indeed, in 2018 Philips was reducing its emphasis on building external connections to HSDP because those efforts were diverting attention from other more important digital efforts. For example, supporting external developers required designing and automating ecosystem partner management and onboarding capabilities. Henk van Houten, Philips's chief technology officer, explained the tension between building internal components versus building the ExDP:

> Commercializing a digital platform externally is not a convincing proposition if you are not migrating your own existing and most successful businesses onto it, solving all implementation difficulties in practice, and demonstrating the end user value. So this is the first priority. It is a bit of a dilemma, as external users will be needed to drive scale.

Schneider Electric has also focused most of its resources on building out EcoStruxure, its internal digital platform. Its occasional use of hackathons allows the company to start taking advantage of partnerships, while the company develops and commercializes internal EcoStruxure offerings. ExDP efforts will surely ramp up over time.

Many executives have told us that they are not interested in building an external developer platform. They are focused on getting benefits from their own digital offerings. Our sense is that, in the early stages of a digital transformation, ignoring an ExDP may be a realistic—even wise—strategy.

Nevertheless, our research has found that all five building blocks, including the external developer platform, are interdependent. The experiences of companies like DBS highlight these interdependencies. The ExDP has placed demands on the company's operational backbone and forced the company to rationalize and further professionalize its digital platform. Like its digital platform, DBS's external developer platform requires attention to prioritization decisions, component ownership, and iterative, Agile methodologies—key characteristics of the company's accountability framework. Finally, customer experiments and insights are important to better understand the intersection between what customers want and what DBS and its external partners can jointly deliver.

Just as an ExDP is dependent on the other building blocks, an ExDP can help build other digital capabilities. For example, an ExDP has unique requirements and can be a natural place to experiment with autonomous teams and accountabilities. It exposes the company to an entirely new set of stakeholders with conflicting and convergent needs, which provides opportunities to build customer insight capabilities. And it can provide useful components that could be added to a digital platform. In other words, a well-managed ExDP will almost certainly boost other building blocks. Unlike the other four building blocks, however, it's hard to even start to build an ExDP unless a company has already developed some capability related to the other four.

Designing and Developing an External Developer Platform

As the DBS, Uber, Royal Philips, and Schneider Electric examples demonstrate, designing an external developer platform to power an ecosystem of developers has the potential to grow revenues, profits, and customer satisfaction.[22] However, we do not recommend that companies guess what kind of external developer platform the world needs and set out to build that platform. Instead, they should first develop a valuable portfolio of reusable components for their own digital offerings. They can then make some of those components available externally as they mature their other digital building blocks.

Building an ExDP takes more than exposing APIs of internal components and cataloging them in a developer portal. Your first challenge will be identifying what kinds of digital components will generate benefits for you, your customers, and your partners. Then, you will need to stimulate external innovation that configures offerings from those components.

> In our survey, the average share of total revenues generated from digital offerings was 5%. Those few companies with a well-developed external developer platform generated, on average, 20% of their revenues from digital offerings.[23]

Identifying which digital components have the greatest potential to provide strategic benefits may be challenging. A component that entails or embeds company-specific data is likely to be uniquely valuable to external parties. Similarly, a component that embeds knowledge or capabilities that your competitors do not possess is likely to be competitively distinctive. On the other hand, any components that are not unique or non-substitutable are commodities, for which there might eventually be a race to the bottom. Ultimately, you want your ExDP to provide access to components that potential partners either do not wish to develop themselves or may not be able to develop in time to meet market demands—and, of course, that enhance their value to customers.

As we've noted, external developer platforms come in two flavors. One involves exposing business and data components that enable partners to create digital offerings leveraging your data or business functionality. The other creates an industry platform exposing infrastructure components that enable partners to add their digital offerings to your marketplace. In both cases, your business partners become customers of your ExDP. You'll need to assign an ExDP owner who will take responsibility in three areas: (1) working with partners to identify valuable components, (2) governing how components are exposed and used, and (3) managing partner relationships.

Getting Your External Developer Platform Right

The external developer platform is just one of five digital building blocks. It probably should not be your first. But bypassing the opportunities that an ExDP offers poses a different competitive risk. And regulations like the open banking requirements in Europe and Australia may force development of an ExDP before a company is quite ready. For most companies an ExDP is likely to be a critical building block. Here is a summary of the key points from this chapter:

- Unless you can provide the best solutions to your customers' every need in a timely manner all by yourself, you will have to tap into the creativity of outside parties as you generate digital offerings. That's why you will need an external developer platform (a managed repository of components that is open to external partners). *Do you already see a need for an ExDP? What benefits will it contribute to your business?*
- You have two options for your external developer platform. One makes business and data components available for external parties to use in developing digital offerings; the other provides an industry platform that serves as a marketplace for distributing multiple companies' digital offerings. *Is your company positioned to deliver on either of these options? What kinds of experiments might help you identify how to drive value from one or both types of ExDP?*
- While an external developer platform will push you to professionalize other building blocks, it relies on having a certain maturity level in the other building blocks. This is why most established companies should not initiate a digital transformation by designing an external developer platform. *Are your other building blocks ready (mature enough) to contribute to an external developer platform?*
- The owner of your external developer platform will take responsibility for working with partners to identify the opportunities and deliver value. This will require business and technical savvy. *Who in your company should take ownership for your ExDP?*

7 Developing a Roadmap for Your Digital Transformation

As you may recall, when Dorothy wanted to go back to Kansas, she had to seek out the Wizard of Oz. It wasn't easy to find the wizard, but at least the path was clear. Follow the yellow brick road.

For established companies that want to go digital, the message is clear: develop five building blocks. Unfortunately, the path is much more cluttered than the yellow brick road. Established companies are sustaining—and improving—their existing businesses as they try to develop digital capabilities. It's not possible to do everything at once. This chapter examines alternative journeys for becoming a digital business.

Assembling the Building Blocks

The digital building blocks reviewed in the last five chapters are organizational capabilities that, according to our research, companies must develop to succeed at digital. To summarize, we have found that a well-designed digital organization has each of the following five capabilities:

- **Shared insights** about what digital solutions the company can develop that customers will pay for (this building block constantly expands knowledge of the intersection between what the company can do with digital technologies and what customers desire).
- An **operational backbone** that captures the company's requirements for integration and standardization of core operational processes (this building block enforces reliability in the execution of foundational processes and integrity of company data).

- A **digital platform** of reusable digital components making up digital offerings (this building block provides access to repositories of business, data, and infrastructure components).
- An **accountability framework** that allocates decision making rights to ensure both autonomy and alignment (this building block defines roles, decision rights, and processes to support speed and alignment in development and use of the digital platform).
- An **external developer platform** that exposes digital components to external partners (this building block provides the technology, processes, and roles enabling digital partner relationships).

Figure 7.1 shows our depiction of the five building blocks for a digital transformation.

Our research confirms that, statistically, the building blocks are five unique, albeit interrelated, organizational assets that contribute individually and in combination to business success.[1] Each building block introduces changes to a company's people, processes, and technology. Consequently, not only is the digital journey long; the series of initiatives to develop any given building block is a journey in itself.

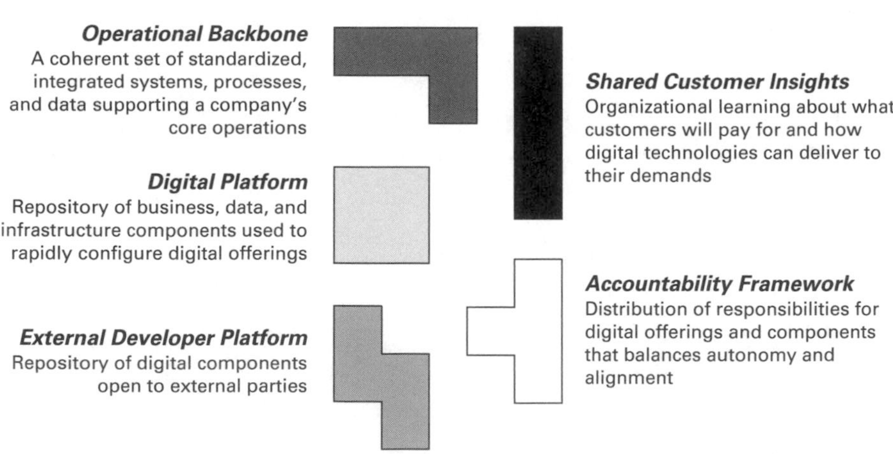

Operational Backbone
A coherent set of standardized, integrated systems, processes, and data supporting a company's core operations
Digital Platform
Repository of business, data, and infrastructure components used to rapidly configure digital offerings
External Developer Platform
Repository of digital components open to external parties
Shared Customer Insights
Organizational learning about what customers will pay for and how digital technologies can deliver to their demands
Accountability Framework
Distribution of responsibilities for digital offerings and components that balances autonomy and alignment

Figure 7.1
The digital building blocks (as introduced in chapter 1)

> A well-developed set of building blocks is related to greater innovativeness of digital offerings and more revenues, profits, and customer satisfaction from those digital offerings.[2]

In a perfect world, companies would be able to develop their building blocks simultaneously—with the possible exception of the external developer platform. Simultaneous development would allow companies to take advantage of the interdependencies among the building blocks. Improving one would improve the others, which would enhance overall benefits.

We have observed, however, that large companies cannot simultaneously address all the building blocks when they kick off a digital transformation. There are too many moving pieces demanding too much organizational change. Thus, leaders must make strategic decisions as to which building block(s) they will focus on at any given time. A transformation roadmap can help sequence development of the building blocks.

Our research suggests that there is no single roadmap that will be optimal for all companies. Companies embark on their digital transformations with different competencies and cultures, and they aim for distinctive futures. What companies have in common is the need to develop the capabilities captured in the five building blocks. Where they differ is in the speed and sequencing of their digital journeys.

For example, leadership at CarMax decided to "spark" a transformation by implementing a new accountability framework that dramatically redesigned work for the subset of people focused on digital offerings. Soon thereafter, CarMax started developing a digital platform. Years ago, USAA started to develop customer insights so that it could provide integrated solutions for members of the US military. Then it redesigned accountabilities so people could deliver those solutions. Philips and Schneider spent years fixing up operational backbones to support core business processes and enable digital initiatives. They followed up those efforts by initiating development of a digital platform. Northwestern

Mutual bought LearnVest, a start-up with an early digital platform, to propel its digital transformation. It then redesigned accountabilities to ensure it could build and leverage digital components.

Given that these different approaches fit well with the needs of the individual companies, we do not propose one optimal digital journey. Instead, we illustrate the different journeys of four companies to give you some ideas about how you can map your company's journey. These companies' digital journeys should help you identify opportunities as they unfold and address the biggest impediments to seizing those opportunities. The most successful companies are pursuing a focused set of capability-building initiatives so that they make steady progress without risking overwhelming organizational changes. The important thing is to get started on the five building blocks. Principal Financial in Chile provides an example of how one company is doing exactly that.

How Principal International Chile Started Its Digital Journey

With its 2,000 employees, Principal International Chile (PI Chile), a subsidiary of Principal Financial Group, focuses on helping its about 800,000 customers become financially ready for retirement.[3] It does so by providing mandatory savings plans, mutual funds for additional voluntary savings, and insurance annuities for retirees.

Chile's pension system requires employees to contribute 10% of their salary to mandatory savings plans. That, however, is insufficient for most people to match their pre-retirement lifestyle upon retirement. PI Chile is committed to using digital offerings to help improve retiree financial security in Chile.

PI Chile has been monitoring digital startups, knowing that customers want easily accessible, simple advice. But its early attempts at becoming digital focused on technology investments. PI Chile Country Head Pedro Atria described the limited impact of this strategy:

> So, we started doing some things here, some things there. We risked having the "shiny toys" syndrome: AI, cloud, mobile, augmented reality. About one year ago, we asked, "Of all these amazing things in the digital world, what would really add value to our customers?"

In September 2017, senior management took a one-week trip to visit Silicon Valley companies. They found themselves in very different kinds of discussions about digital than expected. "All of our discussions had been about strategy, about the vision, about the value proposition, about customers," said Atria. "Because digital is strategy, it's not IT."

After this trip, senior management formulated a new digital strategy. It became *the* business strategy of PI Chile, focusing on using digital technologies to help customers achieve financial security.

Preparing for Digital

As PI Chile embarked on its digital transformation, leaders built on the company's existing operational backbone and the beginnings of a digital platform. The company's operational backbone included two internally developed core systems providing data and functionality around customers and products. The monolithic design of these systems was not perfectly suited for an increasingly digital company, but they offered reliable support for the company's operational processes. PI Chile was also digitizing its customer-focused sales processes as it implemented a cloud-based CRM system.

PI Chile's early digital platform was the foundation for its Principal Connect.cl customer portal. The company had contracted with a local startup to build it; the start-up delivered the first version in just two months. PI Chile leaders viewed their operational backbone and digital platform as a good start to building a digital business, but they also saw the need to create what they call "the muscle," the organizational capabilities required to build digital offerings. As Atria explained,

> We didn't have a digital company. To develop that, we need better data, and we need a different organization, including new talent, different processes, and new, aligned technology. Even our organizational structure ... [is] from an analog world, and we need a structure for the digital world.

Following the announcement of its digital strategy in September 2017, leaders mapped out a transformation journey that focused on the development of two digital building blocks: preparing its *operational backbone* to support digital offerings and initiating changes to *accountabilities* and how people worked.

Developing an Operational Backbone

To quickly enable the development of digital offerings that needed data and functionality from the operational backbone, PI Chile's CIO decided to "wrap" core systems in APIs, that is, to develop APIs to act as intermediaries between the operational backbone and digital offerings. This allows digital offerings to access backbone data or functionality without directly accessing the legacy systems, as those might get replaced in the future.

Top management allocated a budget for developing the first APIs. Two employees in a new, central IT unit coordinated the development of APIs. When digital offering teams saw the need for data or functionality from the operational backbone, they contacted the central API team. The API team checked to see if an API already existed, and if it did not, they designed a new, reusable API. As of mid-2018, the API team had developed around 50 APIs.

Developing an Accountability Framework

To experiment with new ways of working, PI Chile established a new Digital Experience Lab (or DXLab) in 2017. After a nimble start with a handful of employees, the lab had grown to 43 employees by mid-2018. According to the DXLab's director, Daniel Langdon, working there was very different from working elsewhere in PI Chile.

> Everything from how you sit, where you sit, how you collaborate, where you collaborate, what your timetables are, what your perks are, what your organizational structure is, what your career is going to be, etc. In *all* of those dimensions, we are changing radically.

The DXLab was organized into autonomous teams. Each team had at least a product owner with deep understanding of the business problem, a couple of developers, and a designer. Experienced members served as Agile coaches to teams. Every team was also connected to a business sponsor in one of PI Chile's businesses.

Each team was responsible for an offering (such as PrincipalConnect.cl) or a shared component of those offerings (such as a wellness score component that measured a customer's retirement readiness). Teams were organized into "domains." For example, "advice & sales," "fulfillment," and "relationships" were domains; "marketing cloud" was a sub-domain of the "relationships" domain, and "financial planning" was a sub-domain of the "advice & sales" domain. The idea was that domains would have little overlap, so that teams could work as independently as possible.

Another huge shift was that teams stayed responsible for their "product" for its entire life cycle. "A product might eventually die," said Langdon, "but it's more likely to pivot, and if you completely disband the team, you lose all the knowhow, all the information to do that."

Teams, which were called "cells," worked autonomously. Rather than discussing everything with everyone along the hierarchy, teams just made decisions about their "product" themselves. Empowering teams this way located decision making closer to the relevant knowledge. Langdon explained that reliance on empowered teams changed management's role:

> [With hierarchical decision-making] the team first breaks everything down to a few bullet points so that I (as their manager) can make a decision. Then I, the manager without the deep picture, get to ask questions that the team has evaluated for *weeks*. And I start making suggestions that they have already invented, investigated, evaluated against the alternatives, and discarded! We rehash all of those conversations. The only reason that happens is because there's no real confidence, and no real delegation of trust. Instead, what we say *now* is, "this is your domain, this is your playground, and this is what you need to get done." We just build the right culture, build the right team, enable them, delegate the decision-making, and trust the people. And if they have friction, we resolve that friction! Resolving friction is the way I see *my* role.

Langdon made clear to his teams that with this increase in autonomy came increased responsibility:

> You cannot say, "The business didn't give us what we wanted." "The IT people did not respond to us." "The provider didn't ..." No, no, no. All that is all *gone*. You're it.

PI Chile expected to spread the DXLab's ways of working to other parts of the business. Leaders established a handful of Agile cells in other parts of PI Chile focusing on local innovations. DXLab coaches supported these cells. The number of Agile cells was expected to grow quickly.

Developing Additional Building Blocks

Although management focused first on the operational backbone and accountability framework, PI Chile took some early steps to develop its *digital platform* and acquire *customer insights*. Leaders consciously decided against pushing for an *external developer platform* during this time.

As noted, PI Chile had bought an early *digital platform* supporting PrincipalConnect.cl, which the DXLab was extending. The company was also building a new mobile app and various shared digital business components (like the aforementioned wellness score component). At the same time, the DXLab was creating various reusable technical components (like one enabling single sign-on) to its digital platform.

Meanwhile, the DXLab was conducting experiments to gain *customer insights*. Becoming more customer-centric was considered essential, as the company believed that customer insight was more difficult to copy than products. The cells worked in an iterative and incremental way to learn quickly what worked and what did not. Of these experiments, PI Chile's Chief Digital Officer Juan Manuel Vega said,

> We're taking a lot of risks. The DXLab is a space where we can actually *fail*. We're trying different things that we know are going to fail. Failing was not an option eighteen months ago. Today, we *are* failing fast, and fortunately we're failing cheap.

When developing new offerings, DXLab teams sought to learn from customers. For example, when building the first version of the mobile app, customers were asked to use a prototype while being recorded on the smartphone they used. That allowed the team to observe customer reactions. As part of transferring what they were learning about customers, and to get further internal feedback, every Friday the DXLab showcased one of the offerings it was working on.

Looking Ahead

PI Chile leaders are keenly aware that a successful digital transformation requires experimentation. Its transformation roadmap is designed to facilitate that experimentation, according to Roberto Walker, president of Principal Latin America:

> We would like to end up with a digital company end to end. We know also that we are not going to get it right the very first time ... because we know reasonably well what we would like to achieve, but we don't know exactly what it will be like, or what is the best ... or fastest ... way to get there.

In its first year, PI Chile made significant progress on its digital transformation. Figure 7.2 illustrates the authors' interpretation of PI Chile's journey. We reflect the initial investment in each building block with a shape

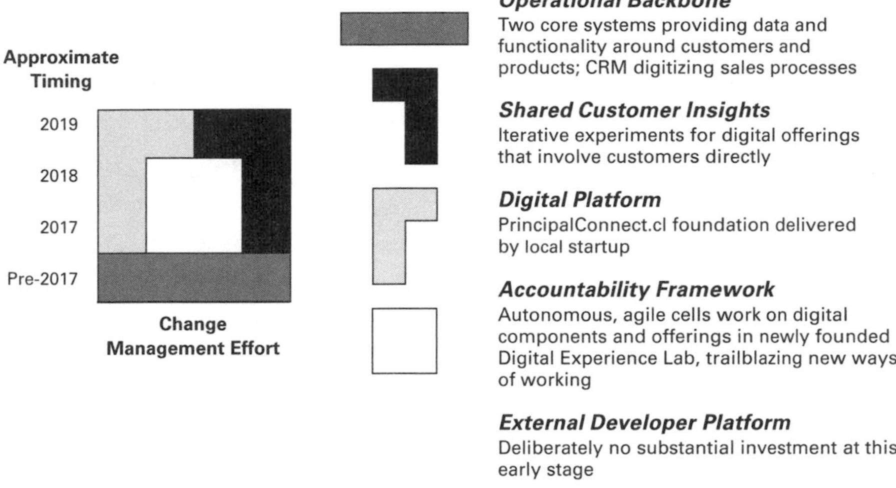
Approximate Timing
2019
2018
2017
Pre-2017
Change Management Effort
Operational Backbone
Two core systems providing data and functionality around customers and products; CRM digitizing sales processes
Shared Customer Insights
Iterative experiments for digital offerings that involve customers directly
Digital Platform
PrincipalConnect.cl foundation delivered by local startup
Accountability Framework
Autonomous, agile cells work on digital components and offerings in newly founded Digital Experience Lab, trailblazing new ways of working
External Developer Platform
Deliberately no substantial investment at this early stage

Figure 7.2
PI Chile's development of digital building blocks (author interpretation)

that reflects the period of time the company initially focused on establishing that building block. As shown, the company first attacked the operational backbone by wrapping key systems in APIs for digital access. The company's accountability framework is the centerpiece of its transformation. By clarifying ownership for customer insights, digital components, and wrapping of operational backbone data, PI Chile is allocating ownership for tasks that will support development of the other building blocks. The DXLab provides a safe environment for PI Chile to develop its building blocks: new accountabilities and ways of working, development of a digital platform, and accumulation of customer insights. Starting with the accountability framework is allowing PI Chile to accelerate its digital transformation. Meanwhile, not diverting resources to an external developer platform helps the company focus on its other building blocks.

Alternative Roadmaps for Building Digital Assets

The PI Chile case highlights both the benefits and the challenges presented by the interdependencies of the building blocks. It is not possible to quickly instill a digital culture and develop digital capabilities in a company that was not born digital. Instead, established companies must accumulate digital capabilities over time.

Part of the challenge in developing any given building block is unlearning old habits and learning new ones. We have found that companies succeed with a building block when they devote significant resources to instituting the new habits required by that building block. For example, companies adopt a test-and-learn approach as they experiment with digital offerings to build customer insights. They invest in adopting standardized processes to build an operational backbone. The digital platform requires companies to create and reuse infrastructure, business, and data components as they build a digital platform. Developing an accountability framework involves assigning empowered and aligned teams to own responsibility for components and offerings. The external developer platform requires developing partnerships that drive additional value from the company's digital platform. Unlearning old habits and learning new habits demands an organizational commitment. That is why it's not possible to develop all building blocks simultaneously.

Successful companies focus initially on developing one or two building blocks. Leaders invest resources to lead the change that will embed a new digital capability. The investment pays off by gradually making the company more agile and enabling progress in the design and delivery of digital offerings. However, progress on any given building block will be thwarted eventually if there is a lack of investment in other building blocks. At some point, leaders need to turn their attention to a different building block to grow the company's digital capabilities.

Because the building blocks are interdependent, a shift in attention does not typically lead to deterioration in earlier building blocks. Rather, any given building block, once it has gained traction, will tend to get stronger as it interacts with other building blocks. Improvements in the accountability framework, for example, help a company ensure the continuous improvement and reuse of the components in its digital platform. Technical and business capabilities built into the digital platform make it possible to carry out experiments that will lead to meaningful customer insights. Customer insights help set priorities for the digital platform, the external developer platform, and even the operational backbone. A building block owner should take responsibility for the constant enhancement of each building block. In this way, companies can grow building blocks individually and as a whole.

Despite the pressures to address all the building blocks all the time, we found that companies made more progress when they took a strategic approach to building one or two blocks. In effect, they followed a roadmap for their critical initiatives to ensure meaningful progress without trying to introduce overwhelming organizational changes. Although the companies we studied did not necessarily have an explicit roadmap, they tended to invest initially in one or two building blocks rather than dabbling in all. These early limited initiatives spawned positive, impactful organizational changes. As is usually the case, focused investments generated faster progress.

> A roadmap can help a company avoid two risks of a digital transformation: (1) dividing resources across so many building blocks that the company doesn't make real progress on any of them or (2) becoming too focused on one or two building blocks for too long and failing to develop other building blocks that are also essential.

To help you define a roadmap that will work for your company, we will describe our interpretation of the journeys of three companies you've learned about throughout the book: Schneider Electric, Philips, and DBS Bank. Each of their journeys reflects their unique competencies and aspirations: by understanding the strategic choices the leaders at these three companies made, we hope to provide insights into the tradeoffs companies encounter and the kinds of strategic decisions that pay off.

The shape of a building block might change from roadmap to roadmap, but the shading stays the same. The building block's shape reflects the company's initial investment in developing it. Some shapes show a focused effort to create a building block in a brief period (i.e., 1–2 years); others show more extended attention over a few years. These shapes are intended to describe how each building block became embedded in the company's organizational design. The task of building these five organizational capabilities is never complete. While the shapes indicate when the company made a commitment to developing a building block, they do not imply that the investment stops when a shape ends.

The individual roadmaps show the authors' interpretation of how each company pieced together all the building blocks. Each company's roadmap highlights which building block(s) served as the starting point for the digital transformation and how management shifted focus to new building blocks as early efforts gained traction. We do not depict all the experiments, the occasional false start, or sustaining investments. Rather we provide a picture of when and how leaders committed to each building block in the company's digital transformation journey.

Schneider Electric

Schneider Electric's digital journey highlights Schneider's unique history and its vision to provide integrated energy management solutions by leveraging the Internet of Things, analytics, cloud, and artificial intelligence.[4] During its long history, Schneider's business had become so complex, that leaders probably had little choice but to invest in an *operational backbone* before trying to develop digital offerings. In 2014, Schneider Electric's leaders started to discuss the business models made possible by the connectivity of customer assets. Though still under construction, the operational backbone that the company had been building for nearly five years had simplified core processes and systems enough to move forward with other building blocks.

Schneider Electric started experimenting with connected products within business units well before the company defined a digital strategy. Initially, the business units retained responsibility for new offerings, as they have with products. Like most companies, however, Schneider found it hard to sell customers on the value of early digital offerings. The company took advantage of strong relationships with a few large global customers who were willing to engage in finding new solutions for their unique energy management needs. This enabled the company to make an early focused investment in accumulating *customer insights*. Since then, Schneider's Digital Services Factory team has adopted innovation approaches that proactively seek customer input.

Schneider Electric's IT leaders recognized the need for a *digital platform* as the company's digital vision unfolded. In particular, they defined what the company refers to as its EcoStruxure platform, intending it to facilitate the connectivity Schneider's digital offerings would demand. IT leaders wanted to get ahead of business demand, so they built into EcoStruxure a set of enabling IoT infrastructure components and some early business components, such as subscription billing. The company has been adding components related to data analytics, including artificial intelligence, and common business components such as dashboarding and automated actions responding to alerts. Schneider now has a large repository of digital components that accelerate development of digital offerings.

As the portfolio of offerings grows, management has been able to shift focus from defining offerings and building core components to getting the accountabilities right. Schneider Electric leaders had recognized their technical challenges before they fully comprehended the organizational changes they needed. Even the Digital Transformation Team initially viewed its challenge as a technical one. More recently, the challenge of leveraging a digital platform across its diverse businesses has focused management attention on getting accountabilities right. A new high-profile digital business unit, established and governed at the executive level under the leadership of a chief digital officer, is taking on the challenge of developing the company's *accountability framework*.

Schneider Electric's foray into external developer partnerships is recent but leaders view its new developer platform as an important strategic initiative. The company has just started to build APIs to enable partners to connect to EcoStruxure components. The company continues to stage hackathons to identify more opportunities to build out its *external developer platform* and expand its marketplace, Schneider Electric Exchange.

Figure 7.3 depicts Schneider Electric's development of its building blocks over the years.

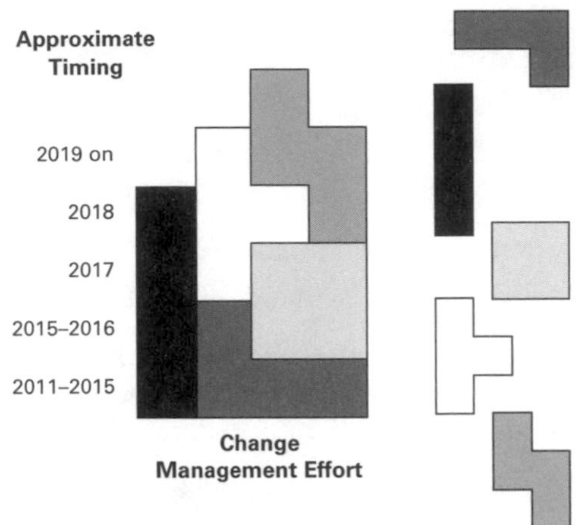

Operational Backbone
A set of 12 ERPs and a global CRM enabling core enterprise processes and master data

Shared Customer Insights
Relationships with key customers to identify and, in some cases, co-innovate valuable offerings

Digital Platform
EcoStruxure: infrastructure components enabling IoT and business and data components configured for intelligent energy solutions

Accountability Framework
Creation of digital business unit to develop and commercialize offerings and provide underlying infrastructure and components

External Developer Platform
Schneider Electric Exchange: development of APIs to engage with external developers and partners in a marketplace

Figure 7.3
Schneider Electric's building block development (author interpretation)

Schneider Electric has benefited from its early start on developing an operational backbone and a digital vision that guided development of key infrastructure components in its digital platform. It has methodically pursued customer insights from valued customers that have produced digital offerings of value to a broader audience. Its external developer platform is expanding its offerings through partnerships.

Schneider leaders still view the status of the operational backbone as an obstacle to digital success. Many old complex companies will feel this pain. For Schneider Electric the greatest challenge is the accountability framework, which will become increasingly important as Schneider builds up its repositories of digital offerings and components. The accountability framework has proved difficult because Schneider is designed around its major business units and because the company is simultaneously building digital capabilities into its physical products—electrical equipment—and its digital offerings. This creates a complex environment for assigning accountabilities. Schneider's digital business unit is trying to coordinate all of its technology efforts. That unit's ability to continue to develop and enhance digital components—and convince business leaders to use them in their offerings—will be key to growing Schneider's digital business.

Royal Philips

Royal Philips's digital transformation began in the later stages of a digitization effort that was designed to turn around a struggling company.[5] In 2014, the company announced its digital strategy: improving healthcare outcomes at lower cost. Its transformation journey has many themes similar to Schneider Electric's.

Philips began its digitization efforts in 2011. By 2014, the company had successfully standardized two of the three processes (idea-to-market and market-to-order) that management felt were core to its business. Work on order-to-cash was still in progress when management attention shifted from the *operational backbone* to developing and commercializing new HealthTech offerings. This shift in focus has allowed Philips to aggressively pursue development of digital offerings, but it has required developing workarounds to support some new business processes, such as subscription billing services. Work on the operational backbone has been ongoing, and, in 2018, leaders are emphasizing the need for enterprise adoption of standardized order-to-cash processes.

Well before Philips initiated its digital transformation, the company had experimented with digital capabilities to create connected products within its product lines. To generate ideas for digital offerings, Philips initially relied on individual business units and on central labs like the Digital Accelerator Lab[6] to accumulate *customer insights*. In 2015, Philips introduced HealthSuite Labs to engage healthcare providers, patients, and payers in intensive workshops to generate ideas for digital offerings that would solve their biggest problems.[7] Philips has since ratcheted up the use of HealthSuite Labs, which—although resource intensive—help generate insights on how potential digital offerings can address customer problems.

IoT, analytics, artificial intelligence, and other digital technologies were at the heart of Philips's digital vision, so the company started to develop HealthSuite Digital Platform (HSDP), a *digital platform* that captured the infrastructure capabilities enabling integration of data from various devices, systems, and other inputs. The company also started building a repository of business capabilities it called CDP². HSDP and

CDP^2 provided reusable components that Philips could then configure into digital offerings. In 2015, Philips developed its first four digital offerings on its platforms. The company had 31 such offerings by 2017 and has been accelerating development of new offerings ever since.

Recognizing the vast number of services required to improve individual health, Philips envisioned early in its transformation that it would need to expand its digital offerings by including partner offerings. As we described in chapter 6, Philips started in 2016 to make HSDP components available via an *external developer platform* for this purpose. In 2018, leaders decided to scale back that effort, however, to concentrate on developing the company's own digital components and offerings. The company continues to offer HSDP access to a small group of partners, and it has launched HealthSuite Insights to provide healthcare specific tools for building, maintaining, deploying, and scaling healthcare-related AI and data science solutions.[8] The scaling back of the ExDP is temporary; it is still an important element of Philips's long-term strategy.

During the company's digitization transformation, the IT unit introduced cross-functional, Agile teams to enhance understanding between IT and business units as the company was implementing its operational backbone. The shift from selling products to developing integrated solutions further required Philips to rethink its *accountability framework*. In 2016 and 2017, Philips experimented with several alternatives ranging from having solution teams as a separate unit to having them more integrated into their market-facing organization. Philips is considering organizing around businesses that provide components and businesses that integrate those components into solutions. It expects its organization to be fluid as it learns what design is most effective.

As figure 7.4 shows, Philips, like Schneider Electric, was actively building an operational backbone even before its digital transformation. When leaders initiated the transformation, they recognized they would also need a digital platform. The building block for customer insights is a particularly challenging one in an industry like healthcare because of the large number of stakeholders (e.g., payers, providers, patients, and

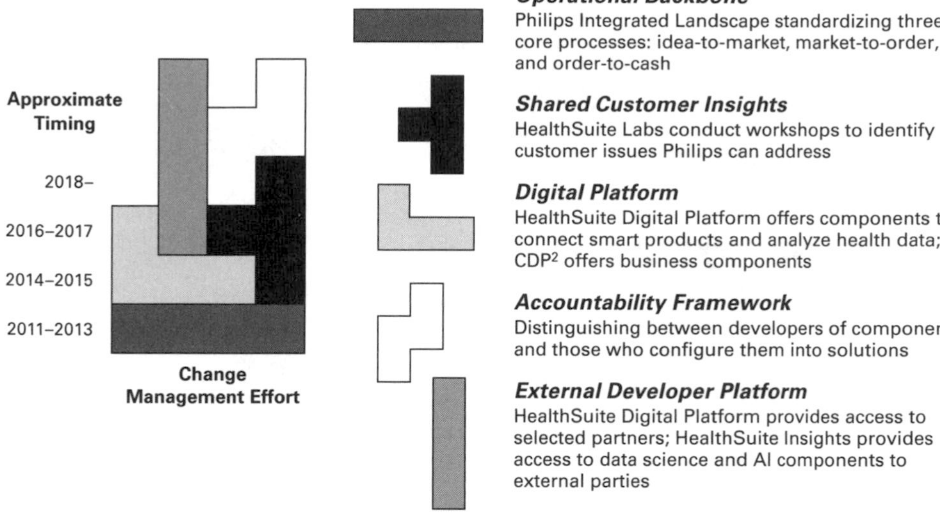
Approximate Timing
2018–
2016–2017
2014–2015
2011–2013
Change Management Effort
Operational Backbone
Philips Integrated Landscape standardizing three core processes: idea-to-market, market-to-order, and order-to-cash
Shared Customer Insights
HealthSuite Labs conduct workshops to identify customer issues Philips can address
Digital Platform
HealthSuite Digital Platform offers components to connect smart products and analyze health data; CDP² offers business components
Accountability Framework
Distinguishing between developers of components and those who configure them into solutions
External Developer Platform
HealthSuite Digital Platform provides access to selected partners; HealthSuite Insights provides access to data science and AI components to external parties

Figure 7.4
Royal Philips's building block development (author interpretation)

policymakers) and because these stakeholders have conflicting goals. HealthSuite Labs is a resource-intensive approach to developing customer solutions that provides deep insights into all stakeholders. Similar to Schneider, Philips is still wrestling with its accountability framework due to the complexity of its business as well as demands to insert digital capabilities into both products (which continue to generate the majority of its revenues) and new digital offerings. It is likely that Philips needs to make progress with its accountability framework before the company can extend broad third-party access to its digital platform. In the meantime, its AI-focused external developer platform will foster learning about how to build, manage, and drive value from third-party relationships.

DBS Bank

As we noted in chapter 2, the digital vision at DBS has evolved over the last decade, but at the core of its vision is a belief that becoming more digital can improve the lives of customers.[9] DBS's earliest initiatives focused jointly on the operational backbone and customer insights.

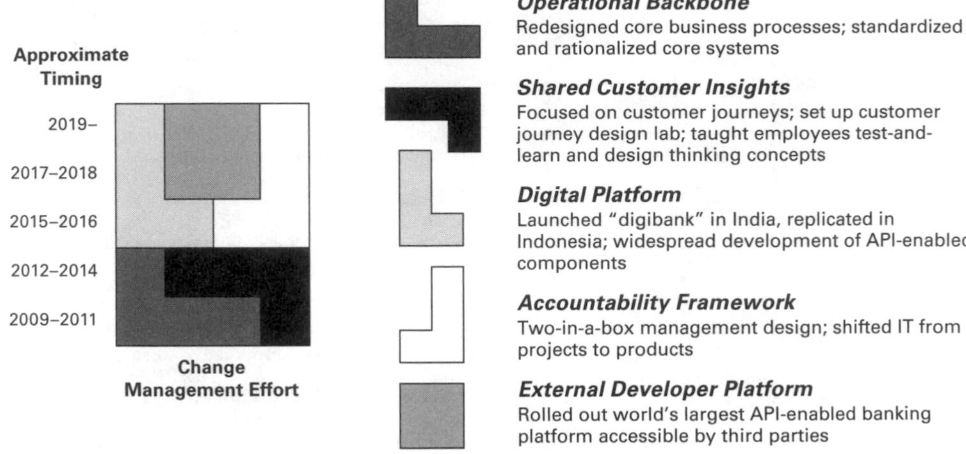
Approximate Timing
2019–
2017–2018
2015–2016
2012–2014
2009–2011
Change Management Effort
Operational Backbone
Redesigned core business processes; standardized and rationalized core systems
Shared Customer Insights
Focused on customer journeys; set up customer journey design lab; taught employees test-and-learn and design thinking concepts
Digital Platform
Launched "digibank" in India, replicated in Indonesia; widespread development of API-enabled components
Accountability Framework
Two-in-a-box management design; shifted IT from projects to products
External Developer Platform
Rolled out world's largest API-enabled banking platform accessible by third parties

Figure 7.5
DBS building block development (author interpretation)

Figure 7.5 depicts our interpretation of the development of building blocks at DBS.

From 2009 to 2014, DBS focused on becoming "digital to the core," transforming its *operational backbone* from fragmented and heterogeneous to standardized and rationalized. This transformation focused on operational excellence and engaged cross-functional teams to redesign core business processes. Process improvement became an organization-wide aspiration when the CEO established a goal of eliminating 100 million wasted customer hours. Employees managed to eliminate 240 million hours by 2014. More recently, DBS has been meeting ambitious goals to radically improve the velocity and reduce the cost of the operational backbone. These efforts have also made operational data and processes readily accessible to digital offerings.

DBS has put considerable emphasis over the last decade on developing *customer insights*. The bank's initial desire to be innovative in the use of digital technology—to be a "22,000-person startup"—shifted quickly to focusing outward, on customers and customer journeys, to provide customers with simple, effortless banking. Starting in 2010, DBS formalized its commitments to both innovation and customer journeys by setting up organizational units to instill these concepts in the entire company. These units have taught test-and-learn concepts, design thinking, and customer journey analysis to most DBS employees. In 2013 the company set up a Customer Journey Design Lab to teach design thinking by doing and has since captured a raft of data from sensors on customer touchpoints so that employees can analyze customer habits and needs. Today, customer journey thinking is pervasive at DBS.

In 2012, DBS seamlessly integrated an internet and mobile services platform for businesses onto its core banking platform. That platform provided straight-through processing and easy access to data for all DBS business customers globally. Recognizing the potential of digital technologies, platform owners within individual business units started developing additional API-enabled components. Although independent business units sometimes duplicated efforts, they built hundreds of digital components. Over time, business units built repositories and created individual *digital platforms*. In 2016, DBS launched an entirely digital bank in India, called "digibank," and reused that platform for a new digital bank in Indonesia a year later.

DBS began experimenting with new ways of working around 2011 with the introduction of new workspaces. About the same time, the company pushed responsibility for customer journeys to individual employees. Since then the company's *accountability framework* has been gradually built on principles of empowerment and evidence-based decision making. In 2018, DBS shifted from projects to products in IT, so that owners of a digital offering take responsibility for its entire life cycle. At the same time, responsibility for developing digital platforms—meaning all the people, technical assets, and budgets that enable a meaningful set of offerings—was devolved to DBS's individual business units. Each business unit's digital platform has dual owners—a technology lead and a business leader—referred to as "two-in-a-box" because the organization chart lists two people. This management approach involves shared missions, goals, resources, metrics, and roadmaps for offerings. Leaders of the platforms receive coaching on how to strategize and manage their new business responsibilities.

As we noted in chapter 6, DBS was motivated to develop its *external developer platform* by the roaring success of a hackathon it organized with startups in 2017. Later the same year, DBS rolled out the world's largest API-enabled banking platform accessible by third parties. The external developer platform is a strategic element of DBS's future growth plans. The strategic importance of the ExDP has motivated the company to rationalize the multiple digital platforms that reside in individual business units.

As a financial institution, DBS is not connecting its digital business to physical products the way Schneider and Philips are. This difference has allowed the company to focus its operational backbone efforts on enhancing customer experience with digital channels and on empowering employees with data. Now, however, the company distinguishes between platforms that support enterprise functions like finance, HR, and legal, and platforms that support products. We refer to the former as the operational backbone and the latter as the digital platform. Distinguishing between these two types of platforms has helped DBS clarify accountabilities for digital offerings and platforms and will facilitate further development of its external developer platform.

One striking element of the DBS story is its extraordinary investment in people. DBS has invested heavily in employee training, mentoring, and skill development, which has instilled a culture of evidence-based decision making. This investment is reaping benefits as the company continues to build and leverage deep customer insights and then convert those insights into valued digital offerings.

Recommendations for Your Digital Roadmap

The four roadmaps we described in this chapter highlight the different approaches companies are taking to their digital transformations. Leaders cannot prioritize everything at once, so they move the needle incrementally on building blocks that are most likely to facilitate a successful transformation.

Although we do not see a single pattern emerging over the four cases in this chapter, we see some generalizable findings about digital roadmaps.

These lead to the following recommendations for developing your roadmap:

Fix the backbone Most established companies find that their *operational backbone* is an impediment to digital success and that they must address its worst deficiencies before they can start to develop digital offerings. Meanwhile, companies with a robust operational backbone can move on to other building blocks. As companies feel an urgency to move forward with digital initiatives, they need to focus strategically on fixing core capabilities that really are essential support for digital business.

Don't put off your digital platform for long Companies usually build some early digital services or offerings before they recognize the need for a *digital platform*. They may simply attach digital components to their operational backbone or they may build a monolithic digital offering. Our sense is that, early on in a digital transformation, this approach can support rapid, local experimentation and learning. It might be a good way to learn about digital value propositions, but pretty quickly companies need to start defining an architecture that supports developing reusable components and offerings. The longer you wait, the more difficult it becomes to create a sustainable technology base for your offerings.

Synchronize your customer insights and digital platform development Some companies start their transformations with a clear picture of what their value proposition for digital offerings will be. They tend to start building *digital platforms* before they have accumulated *shared customer insights*. Other companies work to get to know their customers' demands to help guide development of digital offerings. Our sense is that either approach can succeed and, in the short term, can accelerate development of a single building block. Having a platform of useful components can enable rapid experimentation for customer insights. Conversely, experimentation can help clarify what components are needed. Whichever one they start with, companies need to plan for development of the other, complementary asset. The risk facing companies that move forward on digital platforms without a clear understanding of customer demands is that they can easily invest in components and offerings no one wants—while missing opportunities to create digital offerings that would be valued. The risk of focusing too narrowly on customer insights will be a temptation to respond to those insights by quickly building monolithic offerings that will be very difficult to reuse, scale, or improve.

Start assigning accountabilities The sooner you can adopt an *accountability framework* for digital the better. But it will be difficult to establish accountabilities until you have high-level clarity around digital offerings and components. Balancing autonomy with alignment starts with recognizing the boundaries between distinct living assets. This is especially challenging for engineering companies that have well-established, rigorous, multi-year product development processes. At these companies, software development is located in multiple parts of the company, which will likely complicate both autonomy and alignment. Experiments within innovation labs or the IT unit, particularly experiments that involve iterative, Agile development, can facilitate some early learning.

Don't rush into an ExDP The *external developer platform*, as we mentioned in chapter 6, benefits greatly from the maturity of the other four digital assets. Unless your value proposition relies heavily on building an ecosystem from the start, this building block should wait until the other building blocks are on solid ground.

Keep learning and building Perhaps this goes without saying, but it's probably impossible to simultaneously focus on all five building blocks, at least until some of the building blocks are well established. At the same time, the work on any building block is never complete. The idea is to sequence early development of building blocks based on your most pressing needs. Then develop habits that foster learning and continuous improvement on each individual building block as well as the whole.

You might be wishing for a more explicit plan of attack for your digital transformation than we have provided in this chapter. Be wary, though, if someone offers you such a template. Digital transformations are massive—and still fairly new. Leaders must be prepared to learn what does and doesn't work and adjust course. There is no single path or target business design defining how to become a successful digital business. You need to embark on a journey and allow your digital business to evolve.

We expect that what you'd most like to do is restructure your company to emphasize the growing importance of digital. Indeed, many of the initiatives we cite in this book involve some important new structures like digital business units and customer experience labs. But remember: a digital transformation is mostly *not* about structure. Do not try to succeed in the digital economy with pre-digital approaches!

We are confident that the transformation journey involves developing five digital building blocks: shared customer insights, an operational backbone, a digital platform, an accountability framework, and an external developer platform. The journey is long and the target isn't clear. Nonetheless, our suggestion is: Don't delay building these assets. Get out a napkin and draw your roadmap. *What does your roadmap look like?*

8 Designing Your Company for Digital

In chapter 1, we observed that SMACIT (social, mobile, analytics, cloud, Internet of Things) and other digital technologies are changing the competitive landscape. These technologies have introduced three capabilities that require companies to rethink their customer value propositions: ubiquitous data, unlimited connectivity, and massive automation.

The message of this book is that, to succeed in the digital economy, you need to be inspired by these capabilities. You need to imagine what's now possible for your customers that wasn't possible before. Then you need to design your company—your people, processes, and technologies—to deliver on that inspiration.

There will surely be winners and losers in the digital economy. We anticipate that the winners will succeed at both digital inspiration and digital design. What might not be obvious is that design can—and should—influence inspiration just as much as inspiration influences design: autonomous teams steeped in customer awareness will come up with ideas for offerings you haven't even dreamed of. In this chapter, we'll review how to get digital inspiration and design right.

How *Not* to Be Inspired by Digital Technologies

A risk with digital technologies is that leaders can get caught up in the hype about a technology. In the short term, the value propositions that a given digital technology makes possible typically exceed what any company can pull off. That's because the value realized from the use of digital technologies is limited by what people in complex environments can (and will) actually do.

Without digital (re)design, any new technology will, at best, improve how companies do what they've always done. It won't deliver a new exciting value proposition to customers. For example, big data can provide insights about customer needs. To use those insights, however, someone must be able to adapt an offering to reflect the new knowledge. If a company does not have the appropriate accountability framework around that offering, no one will own—and thus be capable of changing—it. Benefits of big data unrealized!

Similarly, blockchain will deliver data transparency, which can be a powerful business enabler. But companies that have not accumulated insights about what their customers want and what changes they themselves are willing to make may well pursue all kinds of frivolous applications.

This is why the concept of the building blocks is so important. Executives cannot simply insert game-changing technologies into their technology portfolios and wait for valuable new offerings to come rolling out. Companies need to arrange all the pieces of the puzzle so their people will be able to learn how to effectively apply the capabilities of digital technologies to new value propositions.

If a company purposely pursues learning how to (a) build new infrastructure, data and business components, (b) test and learn what its customers value, and (c) enable individuals to deliver on those capabilities while aligning their individual efforts, leaders can take the business to the next level. Artificial intelligence is a perfect example of a technology with lots of potential to change a business—or not.

Artificial Intelligence: Inspiration and Challenge

Perhaps no digital technology generates more excitement about its ability to change business right now than artificial intelligence (AI). Often in conjunction with other digital technologies (especially analytics,

IoT, and cloud computing), AI brings to bear the possibilities that ubiquitous data, unlimited connectivity, and massive automation have to offer. Converting the possibility into reality, however, is not easy.

Autonomous vehicles highlight both the promise and the hiccups that accompany an AI implementation. As with most proposed applications of AI, autonomous driving improves on an old idea—getting a vehicle from one location to another. The opportunities for improvement relate to greater safety (by eliminating human error), lower cost (in cases where the driver is compensated), or elimination of an undesirable manual task (driving, for example, in Bangkok traffic). In other words, AI changes the experience but not the goal.

Conceivably, autonomous vehicles will change the value proposition of automobile manufacturers. They could inspire people to reimagine personal transportation and even lifestyles. But autonomous vehicles must adapt to existing road and transportation systems. If creators of autonomous vehicles could also create the context for autonomous driving, they would build different roads and traffic control systems, and they would propose different rules of the road. But that is not an option.

Autonomous vehicles, for now anyway, must succeed on roads and in systems designed for human drivers. These roads and systems are sometimes unsafe (due to bad design), sometimes inadequate (due to growing usage), and sometimes inefficient (due to changes in travel patterns). These realities mean that autonomous driving features currently constitute product improvements rather than new value propositions.[1] AI algorithms are having an impact on cars—indeed a growing impact—but we haven't realized the dream.

Companies inserting AI into their technology portfolios face a similar challenge. They have existing business models, as well as established processes, systems, and roles. Although the capabilities of AI create opportunities for new business value, a company will only realize that value if it redesigns those systems, processes, and roles and reimagines its value proposition.

Adopting AI for Digitization at OneBankAssure

Leaders at a financial services company, which we will refer to as OneBankAssure (1BA),[2] were inspired by the capabilities of data science and artificial intelligence to transform the company into a more data-driven, customer-centric company. To pursue that vision, in 2014, the CEO created a Decision Science and Machine Learning (DSML) unit and populated it with 30 data scientists and machine learning experts. Three years later, the company had 75 data scientists developing hundreds of new applications a year (90% of which applied machine learning models).

Relative to most of the companies we've studied, 1BA's adoption of AI was extremely successful. AI applications had significant bottom-line impacts and leaders were pleased with the results. They noted, however, that the company had been slow to realize its vision of becoming data-driven and customer-centric. At the time we were studying 1BA, AI had not yet had a meaningful impact on 1BA's customer value proposition. Although a few applications introduced digital customer services (like alerts that a storm is approaching) most of the applications had generated improvements to internal processes and decision-making.

Why had 1BA's AI initiatives fallen short of the vision? Because 1BA had not redesigned its business to drive customer value from AI.

1BA had an excellent operational backbone (which, by the way, had provided invaluable data for AI applications). For the most part, the DSML unit was relying on the same systems and processes 1BA used to build and improve its operational backbone as it implemented AI applications.

Here is the process 1BA used for implementing AI. A steering committee established priorities for data science initiatives and oversaw intermediate outcomes. Although AI project teams were more cross-functional than typical IT development teams (AI teams included a business owner, a user, a data scientist, a business analyst, and, on occasion, a customer), AI teams used essentially the same methodologies for designing and delivering AI applications that produced the company's operational backbone. New code developed by DSML was turned over to IT operations for quality assurance and production, while the DSML experts moved on to their next project. A business owner took responsibility for ensuring that necessary business process changes were adopted. Although the business owner and IT operations shared responsibility for monitoring the behavior of the AI model over time, DSML suggested that models be updated no more frequently than quarterly.

In other words, 1BA was relying on its tried-and-true organizational design and it was generating the kind of business value at which 1BA was proficient. It had not redesigned for digital at the time we were studying it. It had not developed processes for capturing insights about what customers wanted. It had not designed a digital platform to systematize reuse of business, data, and infrastructure components. It had not redesigned accountabilities around living assets. And it had not considered the need for an external developer platform. AI was helping the company generate traditional efficiency benefits, but 1BA had not changed the game! (At least not yet. Its operational backbone will give it a head start when it is ready.) In short, recognizing that a new technology like AI *could* be game changing is not the same as creating the context for a new game.

Customer Value Propositions Inspired by AI

In contrast, at Schneider Electric and Royal Philips—two companies that are substantially designed for digital—AI already forms an integral part of digital offerings.

For example, by inserting AI into its IntelliSpace oncology solutions, Philips helps oncologists monitor changes in a patient's condition (e.g., a growing tumor, a change in weight, an anomaly in a lab test). AI can process data faster than a human, so these AI solutions can offer recommendations on possible therapies that oncologists might have overlooked.[3]

Similarly, Schneider Electric is using AI to improve predictive maintenance.[4] Increasingly, Schneider's customers can rely on AI-powered alerts to tell them when they need to fix or change equipment proactively instead of reactively. These improvements can eliminate breakdowns, unscheduled downtime, and unnecessary onsite service visits.

Philips and Schneider have been able to use AI to enhance—and inspire—customer value propositions because the responsibility for inserting AI components into offerings is owned by the teams that are empowered to continuously improve those offerings. Both companies have mechanisms for accumulating customer insights that identify when a solution would be more valued if it was more intelligent or when a customer problem results from inadequate insights. They have a platform of configurable living assets that can be constantly enhanced without demanding changes in other components. They have an underlying operational backbone (even if it is not as disciplined as they'd like) that enables them to reliably complete transactions and back office processes. They have partners who are expanding their value to customers by developing complementary components and offerings.

DBS applies AI to both internal processes (e.g., deciding which bank branches to audit) and new offerings (e.g., exploiting an AI-enabled chat bot as an enabling feature of its mobile-only bank in India). Its AI expertise is located in AI-focused teams that support or consult to both internal and externally focused teams, as well as in teams that own internal processes and external offerings. DBS is studying how to componentize applications and offerings so that AI models can be isolated from other components. If they can do that, the AI model components can be more dynamic and can learn without requiring changes to other components. This is how AI benefits a company designed for digital.

The capabilities of AI—or any other digital technology or set of technologies—should inspire companies to embark on a transformation journey that will allow them to deliver new value propositions. They may inspire specific ideas of how greater insights could benefit customers. But it's also possible that the inspiration may not offer—at least initially—a very clear vision of where that journey might take them. Part of the transformation journey is learning what your company might achieve for customers, and thus clarifying your vision. Thus, for starters, we don't think companies need to be more inspired than to recognize that digital technologies allow them to fundamentally enrich their customer solutions and engagement. Every company can get started on that journey.

Time to Get Started: A To-Do List for Embarking on Digital Transformation

A surprising number of companies cite the visit of their senior executives to Silicon Valley as the moment they got religion around digital. We are not sure such a trip is the only or best way to get religion. But it is clear that inspired senior leaders are a prerequisite to a successful transformation journey. If a trip to Silicon Valley helps inspire them, take the trip.

But don't expect the trip to Silicon Valley to provide much more than a sense of urgency. It's easy to start flailing when the only thing that's clear is that becoming digital is a competitive necessity. Most leadership teams underestimate the task at hand. So take a pilgrimage, read a book (preferably this one!), hold a leadership team conference, bring in an inspirational speaker—do something to ensure that your leadership team is ready to commit to becoming digital. Then start ticking off the following six items in the to-do list for becoming digital:

1. Choose metrics that inspire people.
2. Assess your building blocks.
3. Roadmap your journey.
4. Establish ownership for each building block.
5. Communicate your vision and your journey.
6. Commit for the long haul.

Choose metrics that inspire people Are you feeling comfortable that quarterly performance metrics and business line financial results will generate passion for your digital transformation? We hope not. You're not serious about digital until you realize that your existing metrics are only relevant to your existing business. Metrics useful for a digital business assess your value to your customer, not your performance. PI Chile seeks to improve customer readiness for retirement. Philips aims to improve healthcare outcomes at lower cost. Schneider Electric is going to make sure customers have all the energy they need for the lowest cost possible. USAA will not be happy until USAA members are financially secure. These goals set companies up to transform. To help your people get excited, they will need some measurable objective. DBS attacked customer-wait time. Philips is going to change three billion lives a year by 2025. Metrics like these change behaviors. In the short term, they also create tension because companies cannot abandon traditional metrics, but companies that establish these metrics and make them count are set up to make progress on their transformation.

Assess your building blocks How strong are your customer insights, operational backbone, accountability framework, digital platform and external developer platform? Recognize your existing capabilities (appendix 2 provides a tool for assessment) so you can build on them. Understand your limitations because they should guide your journey. This assessment will help you prioritize. It will also help people in the company link their own goals to the building blocks. One thing that hasn't changed about strategizing—you still must decide what you're not going to do, not just what you are going to do. Assessing your building blocks will help you identify your highest priorities.

Roadmap your journey Make a plan, even though it will change as you learn what works and doesn't work with customers. Decide what investments matter most now and what needs attention down the road. There will be surprises, but a plan helps you recognize them and adjust. Reevaluate your roadmap regularly by reassessing your building blocks and monitoring your key metrics. In chapter 7, we outlined a way to visualize how you are planning to divide your company's attention and resources across the five building blocks. Go grab some colored sticky notes and start mapping out your company's journey.

Establish ownership for each building block Sometimes everyone in a company shares ownership for a given building block (like customer insight, at DBS). At other times, the owner of a building block (for example, the general manager of your external developer platform, the chief architect of your digital platform, or your CIO) should take it and run with it. Things get done in digital companies when a problem solver takes ownership of a problem and leadership empowers the problem solver to solve it. Building blocks are big commitments. Put a senior leader in charge of each, have that leader define goals and make a roadmap. Then reconcile the roadmaps for the various building blocks, and move forward.

Communicate your vision and your journey Explain your new metrics, expose your building block assessment and roadmap, and make it very clear who owns what. Communicating your intentions will not only help people get on board, it will make it more obvious when the train starts to go off track. Widespread awareness will generate more ideas on how to fix what's broken—and more commitment to doing so.

Commit for the long haul Understand that your board, your investors, and most market analysts are largely clueless about what it means to become digital. Unlike start-ups that accumulate vast sums of investor dollars on what sometimes seems like just the whiff of a good idea, your investors will get nervous when they don't see quarterly results from your digital initiatives. This is no time to hide. State your intentions. Sell your ideas. Communicate your intermediate metrics that will signal progress. Manage expectations. You'll need to sustain your existing business, but you must generate excitement about your vision outside of your organization as well as inside it. As you learn and your roadmap changes, share that too. You're probably not in a position to act like Jeff Bezos, telling people that this is about long-term growth not earnings, but you can take a page from his book. (In his 1997 letter to shareholders, Bezos made the statement that "It's all about the long term." Each year since then, he has attached that letter to his new letters.[5]) Educate your investors, board, employees, and market analysts about what it means to be digital, how you will succeed, and why they should trust you. But also start small. Don't invest massive amounts of resources in ideas that may or may not gain traction. Act like a start-up!

What Are You Waiting for? Design Your Digital Business!

In chapter 1, we acknowledged the temptation to approach strategic change by restructuring the company. We have argued that structure is an inadequate tool. Frans van Houten, CEO at Philips has similarly observed the limitations of structure:

> Historically we have always done a transformation by focusing solely on the organizational structure. For example, we thought that by changing the reporting lines, we would be successful. Of course, this is nonsense and although Philips has reinvented itself many times in the past, I do believe that this narrow approach has held us back. So for our radical transformation to a health technology company, we took a holistic and very comprehensive approach. We integrally addressed all the factors that drive success, including shared vision, culture & behaviors, capabilities, processes & systems, and incentives.

The "factors that drive success" he was referring to are the elements of what we defined in chapter 1 as *digital business design*: the holistic organizational configuration of people (roles, accountabilities, structures, skills), processes (workflows, routines, procedures), and technology (infrastructure, applications) to define value propositions and deliver offerings made possible by the capabilities of digital technologies. The five building blocks described in this book package these elements to deliver that kind of holistic design.

We hope this book has given you the inspiration and confidence to redesign your company for rapid delivery of digital offerings that customers are willing to pay for. It's time to put this book aside and design for digital!

Appendix 1 Committing to an Operating Model to Build an Operational Backbone

In chapter 3, we introduced the operational backbone as the building block companies assemble as they digitize their business processes to create a foundation for efficient and reliable operations. Of the five building blocks, most companies characterize the operational backbone as the biggest obstacle to their digital transformation.[1] That is why this appendix describes a key prerequisite for effectively building an operational backbone: the commitment to an operating model.[2]

What Is an Operating Model?

An *operating model* is the desired level of business process integration and business process standardization for delivering goods and services to customers.[3] Rather than a current state, the operating model describes the target state of how much your business processes should be standardized and integrated.

A standardized business process is performed the same way, no matter where and by whom it is executed. For example, McDonald's is well known for its standardization of operational processes around the globe. Similarly, when CEMEX grew internationally, leaders defined a set of processes, ranging from procurement and finance to logistics and HR, called the "CEMEX Way." Every country organization adopted this enterprise-wide standard way of working.

In contrast, integration is about sharing data among different processes, because they are interdependent: what happens in one business process depends on what happened in another business process. When

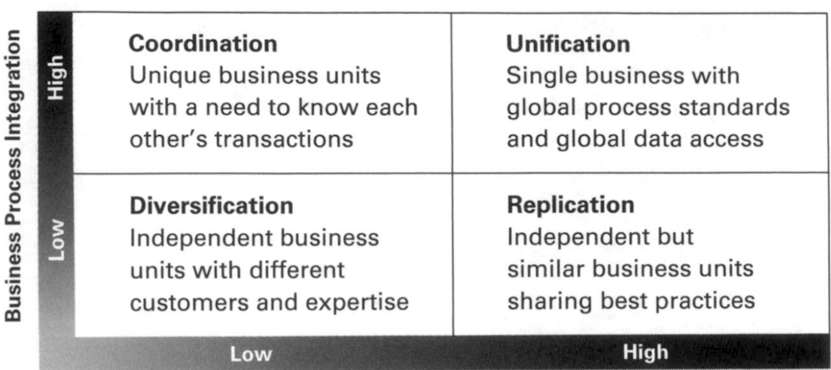

Figure A1.1
Four operating models

one of the authors of this book moved to the US, American Express offered him a credit card even though he had not established a credit history in the US. Since the author had previously owned an American Express credit card in the Netherlands, the company's decision was based on data generated by his past transactions in that country. Obviously, American Express had integrated data from some business processes across the globe.

Recognizing business process standardization and integration as two distinct dimensions, companies can choose from among four different operating models (see figure A1.1):

- **Replication**, characterized by a high desire for standardization, but little need for integration
- **Coordination**, with the opposite requirements: a high need for integration, but not so much for standardization
- **Unification**, with a high need for both standardization and integration
- **Diversification**, characterized by low needs for both standardization and integration

The following examples illustrate the different needs addressed by each operating model.

ING Direct Spain was the first of the ING Direct fleet of country banks to introduce a checking account.[4] When other ING country banks decided to do the same, they first went to Spain to understand how that bank was selling and operating the new product (e.g., how it on-boarded customers) in order to copy their processes. In this way, the countries could learn from each other and share best practices. But if you were a customer of ING Direct Spain and ING Direct Germany, the two banks wouldn't know that because the two banks did not share data. Neither bank's processes would be affected by the fact that you were an ING customer twice over. In other words, ING Direct was following a *replication* operating model: highly standardized processes across countries, but no integration across banks.

When USAA introduced integrated solutions such as Auto-Circle, it needed to share data among different processes.[5] As we described in chapter 1, Auto-Circle combined various financial products like automobile insurance, loans, and buying services into a seamless experience around buying a car. Hence, USAA needed to exchange data among the processes in its different lines of business, such as insurance and banking. But USAA did not require standardizing processes across these lines of business, partly because of different regulatory requirements and partly because of different product features. USAA was following a *coordination* operating model.

When DHL Express set out to turn around its international shipping business in the US, it decided it needed both business process integration and standardization.[6] For example, it wanted its global customers to be able to track a shipment from the US to Brazil even when calling a customer service center in Singapore. That required data sharing. To ensure the integrity of the data and the predictability of the process, DHL also wanted to adopt in the US the standardized logistics processes like inbound and outbound package handling that had been adopted in other countries. Hence, DHL Express followed a *unification* operating model.

Portfolio companies like Berkshire Hathaway don't need integration among the different companies in their portfolio (in fact, integration would hinder any attempts to sell a company quickly). Such companies also have little need to standardize their core business processes. This is why they pursue a *diversification* operating model.

How to Choose among Operating Models

Each operating model is a valid choice; no model is superior. Instead, with each operating model, companies can expect certain benefits, while forgoing others. Through standardization, replication promises consistency that ensures the same transaction quality across different countries or units. It facilitates efficiencies at the cost of differentiation. It also offers scale benefits: the same processes (and the systems supporting them) are reused multiple times. A related benefit is that employees can easily transfer to different company locations.

Because it is concerned with standardization and not integration, the replication model does not offer a single cross-unit view of, say, customers. That is a key benefit of the coordination operating model. Companies adopt a coordination operating model so they can serve customers across business silos while enabling differentiation of products and services across different parts of the company. Because they do not standardize processes, however, companies choosing the coordination operating model find it can be costly to maintain. It enables customer intimacy but sacrifices efficiency.

Unification, of course, combines the best of replication and coordination: efficiency and enterprise-wide view of key data. Unification, however, sacrifices local responsiveness and the ability to customize for individual segments, lines of business, or geographies. For companies selling commodity products, unification facilitates operational efficiency. But if a company wants to avoid commoditization, the unification operating model is a bad choice.

The diversification operating model maximizes local innovation. It enables business units to grow independently. With fewer constraints, business units in a company adopting a diversification operating model can experiment locally and quickly implement innovations that respond to customer needs. Although some companies adopting a diversification operating model introduce enterprise shared services to generate economies of scale, these systems and processes are hard to adopt because local business leaders are accustomed to autonomy. Some shared services around non-distinctive processes make business sense, but they can be difficult to implement.

Readers should note that complex companies have to make operating model decisions on multiple levels. For example, a company's operating model on the corporate level (e.g., the degree of integration and standardization across various business units) can be different from its operating models at the business unit level (e.g., the degree of integration and standardization across regions within a given business unit).

How Does an Operating Model Relate to Building an Operational Backbone?

Building an operational backbone demands a commitment to an operating model. If a company does not choose an operating model, every IT investment cycle will find the company pursuing immediate concerns rather than building long-term capabilities. IT and change management decisions will lack coherence. Thus, companies that want local responsiveness but insist on implementing global ERPs with standardized processes will find the outcomes frustrating. Meanwhile, companies attempting to create a single view of customers but adopting a diversification model will never get that single view.

You need not adopt a pure operating model (for example, you can decide that customer data must be integrated but product data need not be), but you must commit to the operating model you choose. How do you plan to profit and grow? Do you need local responsiveness more than scale benefits? Do you need to have an integrated view of the customer? Do you need to ensure consistency across your businesses?

Choosing an operating model helps companies focus their systems and process change investments on the most essential aspects of their operational backbone. For example, for the replication model, enterprise systems like ERPs and product life cycle management systems can provide the systems support for standardized processes. Because replication doesn't require data sharing, these enterprise systems can be defined and implemented at the business unit level.

Unification, in contrast, requires that such systems be adopted globally. The coordination model requires shared access to central data. Companies often adopt CRMs to standardize their data capture and user interfaces. Companies with diversification models implement systems best suited to the individual businesses (except where the company attempts to drive efficiencies by standardizing non-distinctive shared services).

The value of the operating model is that it defines the default choice for the questions of standardization and integration. For example, in a replication model, when facing the decision of whether to follow a standard process or leave room for local responsiveness, the default answer is to follow the standard, but for a given process, there may be good reasons to deviate. Without this agreed-upon default decision, every IT investment decision requires an organizational justification. A company with a default operating model need only debate requests for exceptions.

Some companies find themselves trying to deliver integrated solutions to customers when their business units are silos hoarding their own, inconsistent data, and supporting many variations of a business process. Conversely, other companies are wasting money trying to implement enterprise systems when they have designed governance and incentives for local innovation. A commitment to an operating model provides consistency between investments and capabilities.

Deciding on an operating model is a strategic commitment that cannot be changed easily. Switching to another operating model (or establishing one in the first place) involves changing how people are working and how systems are interacting. The operating model affects roles, incentive systems, and skills. For example, when Royal Philips standardized global business processes, leaders introduced executive business process owners (at the level of the executive committee) to enforce these standards. The IT unit stopped asking business unit leaders for their requirements and interacted mostly with business process owners, who were responsible for aggregating requirements from different units.[7] Philips did business differently after changing the company's operating model. This is why digitizing your processes with an operational backbone is a business transformation. This is also why it's hard.

Committing to an operating model is the first step in building your operational backbone. We anticipate it will also help companies define how they approach their digital platform building block. Specifically, a diversified company will build multiple digital platforms—one for each autonomous business, while a company with a unification operating model will surely want just one. Replication and coordination companies likely have choices on how to design their digital platforms, particularly if they have a robust operational backbone. Figure A1.1 can help you start the discussion on what operating model will work best for you.

Appendix 2 Assessing Your Building Blocks for Digital Transformation

This appendix offers an assessment tool companies can use to gauge their progress on the digital transformation journey. The assessment tool borrows from a survey we distributed from May to August 2018. The results of the survey are available online at cisr.mit.edu.[1] To maximize the value of this assessment, leaders should complete the survey individually and discuss differences in their assessments.

To start, use the building block definitions in figure 1.1 to rate the current status of each of your enterprise's digital building blocks:

	Non-existent (1)	Limited Investment/ Experiments (2)	Expanding Investment/ Experiments (3)	Committed and Rolling Out (4)	Widely Adopted and Valuable (5)
a. Shared Customer Insights	○	○	○	○	○
b. Operational Backbone	○	○	○	○	○
c. Digital Platform	○	○	○	○	○
d. Accountability Framework	○	○	○	○	○
e. External Developer Platform	○	○	○	○	○

Now examine each building block in more detail using the following questions:

Your enterprise's ***current* knowledge about the value of digital to customers ...**

	Strongly Disagree (1)	Disagree (2)	Somewhat Disagree (3)	Agree and Disagree (4)	Somewhat Agree (5)	Agree (6)	Strongly Agree (7)
a. Stems from a constant flow of experiments/small initiatives that help identify what customers value	○	○	○	○	○	○	○
b. Is built on experiments/small initiatives that explore what digital technologies can do	○	○	○	○	○	○	○
c. Is guided by a vision that targets a new customer value proposition	○	○	○	○	○	○	○
d. Is enhanced by tightly integrated sales, service, and product development processes	○	○	○	○	○	○	○
e. Is enhanced by customer co-creation processes for digital offerings	○	○	○	○	○	○	○
f. Is enhanced by mechanisms for sharing learning from experiments/small initiatives across the enterprise	○	○	○	○	○	○	○

Your underlying operational backbone—the systems (e.g., ERP, CRM), processes, and data supporting your core transactions—*currently* …

	Strongly Disagree (1)	Disagree (2)	Somewhat Disagree (3)	Agree and Disagree (4)	Somewhat Agree (5)	Agree (6)	Strongly Agree (7)
a. Supports seamless end-to-end transaction processing	○	○	○	○	○	○	○
b. Provides visibility into transactions (or, if you have few transactions, visibility into core operations)	○	○	○	○	○	○	○
c. Automates repetitive business processes	○	○	○	○	○	○	○
d. Provides a single source of truth	○	○	○	○	○	○	○

Your digital platform—the business, data, and infrastructure components facilitating rapid innovation and enhancement of digital offerings—*currently* …

	Strongly Disagree (1)	Disagree (2)	Somewhat Disagree (3)	Agree and Disagree (4)	Somewhat Agree (5)	Agree (6)	Strongly Agree (7)
a. Provides a repository of reusable technical components	○	○	○	○	○	○	○
b. Provides a repository of reusable business components	○	○	○	○	○	○	○
c. Includes data repositories and tools supporting analytics	○	○	○	○	○	○	○

(*continued*)

	Strongly Disagree (1)	Disagree (2)	Somewhat Disagree (3)	Agree and Disagree (4)	Somewhat Agree (5)	Agree (6)	Strongly Agree (7)
d. Offers linkages to core data and processes in your operational backbone	○	○	○	○	○	○	○
e. Facilitates continuous release of new components	○	○	○	○	○	○	○
f. Is enhanced by mechanisms you have formalized for identifying reusable components	○	○	○	○	○	○	○

Your **accountability framework**—that is, the individuals or teams accountable for digital components and offerings—*currently* …

	Strongly Disagree (1)	Disagree (2)	Somewhat Disagree (3)	Agree and Disagree (4)	Somewhat Agree (5)	Agree (6)	Strongly Agree (7)
a. Are organized around digital components and offerings rather than business units, disciplines, or functions	○	○	○	○	○	○	○
b. Have clear accountabilities enabling a high degree of autonomy	○	○	○	○	○	○	○
c. Establish their own metrics for achieving stated objectives/mission	○	○	○	○	○	○	○

	Strongly Disagree (1)	Disagree (2)	Somewhat Disagree (3)	Agree and Disagree (4)	Somewhat Agree (5)	Agree (6)	Strongly Agree (7)
d. Release their own code into production when they deem appropriate	○	○	○	○	○	○	○
e. Have access to the resources they need to accomplish their objectives	○	○	○	○	○	○	○
f. Make their own decisions based on data/evidence	○	○	○	○	○	○	○

Your external developer platform—a platform for an ecosystem of partners who contribute and use digital components—*currently* …

	Strongly Disagree (1)	Disagree (2)	Somewhat Disagree (3)	Agree and Disagree (4)	Somewhat Agree (5)	Agree (6)	Strongly Agree (7)
a. Makes components available to external partners	○	○	○	○	○	○	○
b. Supports inclusion of external partner components into your enterprise's digital offerings	○	○	○	○	○	○	○
c. Publishes the catalog of digital services available to partners	○	○	○	○	○	○	○
d. Has automated the onboarding of external partners on the platform	○	○	○	○	○	○	○

Notes

Chapter 1

1. J. C. Anderson, J. A. Narus, and W. van Rossum, "Customer Value Propositions in Business Markets," *Harvard Business Review* 84, no. 3 (March 2006): 90–99.

2. M. Mocker, J. W. Ross, and C. Hopkins, "How USAA Architected its Business for Life Event Integration," *MIS Quarterly Executive* 14, no. 4 (2015).

3. AUDI's experiments are described in more detail in M. Mocker and N. O. Fonstad, "How AUDI AG is Driving Toward the Sharing Economy," *MIS Quarterly Executive* 16, no. 4 (2017).

4. C. F. Gibson, "Turnaround at Aetna: The IT Factor," MIT Sloan Center for Information Systems Research, Working Paper No. 362, August 2006; J. W. Ross and C. M. Beath, "Campbell Soup Company: Harmonizing Processes and Empowering Workers," MIT Sloan Center for Information Systems Research, Working Paper No. 374, June 2008; R. Chung, D. Marchand, and W. Kettinger, "The CEMEX Way: The Right Balance Between Local Business Flexibility and Global Standardization," IMD Case 3–1341, 2005, and also R. Chung, K. Paddack, and D. Marchand, "CEMEX: Global Growth Through Superior Information Capabilities," IMD Case 3–0953, 2003; M. Mocker, J. W. Ross, and P. Ciano, "DHL Express: Implementing and Maintaining a Global Process Standard," MIT Sloan Center for Information Systems Research, Working Paper No. 393, January 2014; P. Andersen and J. W. Ross, "Transforming the LEGO Group for the Digital Economy," MIT Sloan Center for Information Systems Research, Working Paper No. 407, March 2016; J. W. Ross and C. M. Beath, "USAA: Organizing for Innovation and Superior Customer Service," MIT Sloan Center for Information Systems Research, Working Paper No. 382, December 2010.

5. For research on the relationship between business transformations and business performance, see E. Brynjolfsson and L. M. Hitt, "Beyond

Computation: Information Technology, Organizational Transformation and Business Performance," *Journal of Economic Perspectives* 14, no. 4 (Fall 2000): 23–48.

6. J. W. Ross, P. Weill, and D. Robertson, *Enterprise Architecture as Strategy: Creating a Foundation for Business Execution* (Harvard Business School Press, 2006).

7. Our discussion of Amazon draws on Brad Stone, *The Everything Store: Jeff Bezos and the Age of Amazon* (Little, Brown and Co, 2013); Robert Spector, *Amazon.com: Get Big Fast* (Harper Collins, 2009); Frank Rothaermel, "Amazon.com, Inc., McGraw Hill Case, MH0053," May 25, 2017; and H. Sender, L. Stevens, and Y. Serkez, "Amazon: The Making of a Giant," *The Wall Street Journal*, March 14, 2018. Available at: http://www.wsj.com/graphics/amazon-the-making-of-a-giant/ (accessed August 2, 2018).

8. R. Borison, "Here Are 10 of Amazon's Biggest Failures," thestreet.com, November 15, 2015. Available at: https://www.thestreet.com/story/13364106/1/here-are-10-of-amazon-s-biggest-failures.html (accessed August 25, 2018).

9. The description of Philips's transformation is based on M. Mocker and J. W. Ross, "Transforming Royal Philips to Reinvent Healthcare in the Digital Age," MIT Sloan Center for Information Systems Research, Working Paper No. 425, December 2017; and J. W. Ross, M. Mocker, and E. Van Zoelen, "Architecting a Digital Transformation at Royal Philips," MIT Sloan Center for Information Systems Research, Research Briefing, January 2018.

10. Philips's method for counting how many lives they are improving each year can be found here: "Sustainability: Today We Are Improving the Lives of Every 4th Person on Earth," philips.com, (no date). Available at: https://www.philips.com/a-w/about/sustainability/lives-improved.html (accessed October 25, 2018).

Chapter 2

1. Wikipedia contributors, "Christopher Columbus," *Wikipedia, The Free Encyclopedia*. Available at: https://en.wikipedia.org/w/index.php?title=Christopher_Columbus&oldid=865606389 (accessed October 25, 2018).

2. Biz Carson, "How 3 Guys Turned Renting an Air Mattress in Their Apartment into a $25 Billion Company," business insider.dot com, Feb 23, 2016. Available at: https://www.businessinsider.com/how-airbnb-was-founded-a-visual-history-2016-2 (accessed October 15, 2018).

3. Megan Garber, "Instagram Was First Called "Burbn," theatlantic.com, July 2, 2014. Available at: https://www.theatlantic.com/technology/archive/2014/07/instagram-used-to-be-called-brbn/373815/ (accessed October 15, 2018).

4. Nicholas Carlson, "The Real History of Twitter," businessinsider.com, April 13, 2011. Available at: https://www.businessinsider.com/how-twitter-was-founded-2011-4 (accessed October 15, 2018).

5. "Audi closes down its Stockholm-based pilot project for car sharing," nordic9.com, February 10, 2017. Available at: https://nordic9.com/news/audi-closes-down-its-stockholm-based-pilot-project-for-carpooling-news5528109642/(accessed October 15, 2018; and Andrew Krok, "Audi On Demand car sharing program launches in UK," cnet.com, August 20, 2018. Available at: https://www.cnet.com/roadshow/news/audi-on-demand-car-sharing-uk/ (accessed October 15, 2018).

6. N. O. Fonstad and J. W. Ross, "Learning How to Test and Learn," MIT Sloan Center for Information Systems Research, Research Briefing Vol. XVI, No. 2, February 2018.

7. J. W. Ross, C. M. Beath, and K. Moloney, "Schneider Electric: Connectivity Inspires a Digital Transformation," MIT Sloan Center for Information Systems Research, Working Paper No. 417, May 2017.

8. R. C. McGrath and I. C. MacMillan, *Discovery-Driven Growth: A Breakthrough Process to Reduce Risk and Seize Opportunity* (Harvard Business Review Press, 2009).

9. M. Mocker, J. W. Ross, and C. M. Beath, "How Companies Use Digital Technologies to Enhance Customer Offerings—Summary of Survey Findings," MIT Sloan Center for Information Systems Research, Working Paper No. 434, February 2019.

10. "CEMEX Delivers the Future: CEMEX Go," press release, November 6, 2017. Available at: https://www.cemexusa.com/-/cemex-delivers-the-future-cemex-go (accessed October 8, 2018).

11. See P. Gupta, "Our Digital Strategy," dbs.com, November 17, 2017. Available at: https://www.dbs.com/investorday/presentations/Our_digital_strategy.pdf (accessed August 25, 2018).

12. S. K. Sia, C. Soh, and P. Weill, "How DBS Bank Pursued a Digital Business Strategy," *MIS Quarterly Executive* 15, no. 2 (June 2016): 105–121.

13. Ibid.

14. Gordon Platt, "World's Best Bank Awards 2018: DBS Named Best Bank in the World," *Global Finance Magazine*, October 1, 2018. Available at: http://www.gfmag.com/magazine/october-2018/worlds-best-banks-2018 (accessed October 18, 2018).

15. P. Betancourt, J. Mooney, and J. W. Ross, "Digital Innovation at Toyota Motor North America: Revamping the Role of IT," MIT Sloan Center for Information Systems Research, Working Paper No. 403, September 2015.

16. M. Mocker and J. W. Ross, "ING Direct Spain: Managing Increasing Complexity while Offering Simplicity," MIT Sloan Center for Information Systems Research, Working Paper No. 390, June 2013.

17. See M. Mocker and J. W. Ross, "The Problem with Product Proliferation," *Harvard Business Review* 95, no. 3 (2017): 104–110; and M. Mocker, J. W. Ross, and K. Kosgi, "Mastering Business Complexity: MIT CISR Survey Results," MIT Sloan Center for Information Systems Research, Technical Research Report, Working Paper No. 405, February 2016.

18. N.O. Fonstad and J. W. Ross, "Ferrovial: Leveraging Internal and External Resources to Innovate Competitively," MIT Sloan Center for Information Systems Research, Working Paper No. 409, March 2016.

Chapter 3

1. J. W. Ross, I. Sebastian, C. M. Beath, and L. Jha, "Designing Digital Organizations—Summary of Survey Findings," MIT CISR Working Paper No. 415, February 2017; and M. Mocker, J. W. Ross, and C. M. Beath, "How Companies Use Digital Technologies to Enhance Customer Offerings—Summary of Survey Findings," MIT Sloan Center for Information Systems Research, Working Paper No. 434, February 2019.

2. J. W. Ross, I. Sebastian, C. M. Beath, and L.Jha, "Designing Digital Organizations—Summary of Survey Findings."

3. J. W. Ross, C. Beath, and I Sebastian, "Why Nordstrom's Digital Strategy Works (and Yours Probably Doesn't)," hbr.org, January 14, 2015. Available at: https://hbr.org/2015/01/why-nordstroms-digital-strategy-works-and-yours-probably-doesnt (accessed August 26, 2018).

4. The case of CEMEX is described in more detail in J. W. Ross, P. Weill, and D. C. Robertson, *Enterprise Architecture as Strategy* (Harvard Business School Press, 2006), 177–179.

5. M. Kagan, I. Sebastian, and J. W. Ross, "Kaiser Permanente: Executing a Consumer Digital Strategy," MIT Sloan Center for Information Systems Research, Working Paper No. 408, March 2016.

6. See "Kaiser Permanente Again Tops Annual Consumer Loyalty Study," kaiserpermanente.com, press release, June 12, 2018. Available at: https://share.kaiserpermanente.org/article/kaiser-permanente-again-tops-annual-consumer-loyalty-study/ (accessed July 24, 2018).

7. M. Mocker, J. W. Ross, and C. M. Beath, "How Companies Use Digital Technologies."

8. P. Andersen and J. W. Ross, "Transforming the LEGO Group for the Digital Economy," MIT Sloan Center for Information Systems Research, Working Paper No. 407, March 2016.

9. K. Oliver, E. Samakh, and P. Heckmann, "Rebuilding Lego, Brick by Brick," strategy+business, August 29, 2007. Available at: https://www.strategy-business.com/article/07306 (accessed May 3, 2018).

10. D. Robertson and B. Breen, *Brick by Brick: How LEGO Rewrote the Rules of Innovation and Conquered the Global Toy Industry* (Crown Business, 2014).

11. D. Hannon, "LEGO Builds a Broader Product Line with SAP PLM," SAPinsider, April 1, 2012. Available at: https://sapinsider.wispubs.com/Assets/Case-Studies/2012/April/LEGO-Builds-A-Broader-Product-Line-With-SAP-PLM (accessed October 8, 2018).

12. J. W. Ross and C. Beath, "Campbell Soup Company: Harmonizing Processes and Empowering Workers," MIT Sloan Center for Information Systems Research, Case Study, Working Paper No. 374, June 2008.

13. M. Mocker, J. W. Ross, and P. Ciano, "DHL Express: Implementing and Maintaining a Global Process Standard," MIT Sloan Center for Information Systems Research, Case Study, Working Paper No. 393, January 2014.

14. M. Kagan, I. M. Sebastian, and J. W. Ross, "Kaiser Permanente: Executing a Consumer Digital Strategy," MIT Sloan Center for Information Systems, Working Paper No. 408, March 2016.

15. B. Wixom and J. W. Ross, "The US Securities and Exchange Commission: Working Smarter to Protect Investors and Ensure Efficient Markets," MIT Sloan Center for Information Systems Research, Working Paper No. 388, November 2012.

16. M. Mocker, J. W. Ross, and E. Van Heck, "Transforming Royal Philips: Seeking Local Relevance While Leveraging Global Scale," MIT Sloan Center for Information Systems Research, Case Study, Working Paper No. 394, February 2014; and M. Mocker and J.W. Ross, "Transforming Royal Philips to Reinvent Healthcare in the Digital Age," MIT Sloan Center for Information Systems Research, Working Paper No. 425, December 2017.

17. For a detailed discussion of how to define and implement an operating model, please refer to J. W. Ross, P. Weill, and D. C. Robertson, *Enterprise Architecture as Strategy* (Harvard Business School Press, 2006).

18. M. Mocker, J. W. Ross, and C. M. Beath, "How Companies Use Digital Technologies."

19. M. Mocker and J. W. Ross, "The Problem with Product Proliferation," *Harvard Business Review* 95, no. 3 (2017): 104–110.

20. Ibid.

21. M. Mocker and J. W. Ross, "ING Direct Spain: Managing Increasing Complexity while Offering Simplicity," MIT Sloan Center for Information Systems Research, Working Paper No. 390, June 2013.

22. J. W. Ross, "United Parcel Service: Delivering Packages and e-Commerce Solutions," MIT Sloan Center for Information Systems Research, Working Paper No. 318, August 2001.

23. A. Karunakaran, J. Mooney, and J. W. Ross, "Accelerating Global Digital Platform Deployment Using the Cloud: A Case Study of Schneider Electric's 'bridge Front Office' Program," MIT Sloan Center for Information Systems Research, Working Paper No. 399, January 2015.

24. N. O. Fonstad and J. W. Ross, "Building Business Agility: Cloud-Based Services and Digitized Platform Maturity," MIT Sloan Center for Information Systems Research, Research Briefing Vol. XV, No. 2, February 2015.

Chapter 4

1. P. Andersen and J. W. Ross, "Transforming the LEGO Group for the Digital Economy," MIT Sloan Center for Information Systems Research, Working Paper No. 407, March 2016.

2. Based on A. Marshall, "Lyft Redesigns its App—and Strategy—for the Age of Sharing," *Wired*, June 7, 2018. Available at: https://www.wired.com/story/lyft-app-redesign-sharing/ (accessed August 3, 2018); and Wikipedia contributors, Lyft, *Wikipedia, The Free Encyclopedia*. Available at: https://en.wikipedia.org/w/index.php?title=Lyft&oldid=851918209 (accessed August 3, 2018).

3. "Toyota Launches Car Share Service in Honolulu through Servco Pacific Inc.," toyota.com, press release, July 10, 2018. Available at: https://pressroom.toyota.com/releases/toyota+launches+car+share+service+in+honolulu+through+servco+pacific.htm (accessed October 8, 2018).

4. This comparison is based on I. Sebastian, J. W. Ross, C. M. Beath et al., "How Big Old Companies Navigate Digital Transformation," *MIS Quarterly Executive* (2017).

5. J. W. Ross, I. Sebastian, C. M. Beath et al., " Designing Digital Organizations—Summary of Survey Findings," MIT Sloan Center for Information Systems Research, Working Paper No. 415, February 2017.

6. M. Mocker, J. W. Ross, and C. M. Beath, "How Companies Use Digital Technologies to Enhance Customer Offerings—Summary of Survey Findings," MIT Sloan Center for Information Systems Research, Working Paper No. 434, February 2019.

7. J.W. Ross, I. Sebastian, C.M. Beath et al, "Designing Digital Organizations—Summary of Survey Findings," and M. Mocker, J.W. Ross, and C.M. Beath, "How Companies Use Digital Technologies to Enhance Customer Offerings—Summary of Survey Findings."

8. J. W. Ross, C. M. Beath, and K. Moloney, "Schneider Electric: Connectivity Inspires a Digital Transformation," MIT Sloan Center for Information Systems Research, Working Paper No. 471, May 2017.

9. This quote is from M. Mocker and J. W. Ross, "Transforming Royal Philips to Reinvent Healthcare in the Digital Age," MIT Sloan Center for Information Systems Research, Working Paper No. 425, December 2017.

10. M. Mocker, J. W. Ross, and C. M. Beath, "How Companies Use Digital Technologies."

11. J. W. Ross, I. M. Sebastian, and C. M. Beath, "BNY Mellon: Redesigning IT for Digital Transformation," MIT Sloan Center for Information Systems Research, Working Paper No. 416, April 2017.

12. C. M. Beath, I. M. Sebastian, and J. W. Ross, "Northwestern Mutual's Digital Transformation: Redesigning IT," MIT Sloan Center for Information Systems Research, Working Paper No. 423, October 2017.

13. M. Raskino, "Techquisitions: An Uncommon Approach Some CEOs Use for Digital Business Acceleration," Gartner White Paper G00292866, October 27, 2015.

Chapter 5

1. J. W. Ross, C. M. Beath, and I. M. Sebastian, "BNY Mellon: Redesigning IT for Digital Transformation," MIT Sloan Center for Information Systems Research, Working Paper No. 416, April 2017.

2. Christopher Null, "10 Companies Killing It at DevOps," *Techbeacon*, (no date). Available at: https://techbeacon.com/10-companies-killing-it-devops (accessed on August 13, 2018).

3. L. Bass, I. Weber, and L. Zhu, *DevOps: A Software Architect's Perspective* (Addison-Wesley Professional, 2015), 4.

4. Steve Urban, "Netflix's 'Context, Not Control': How Does It Work?" linkedin.com, August 20, 2015. Available at: https://www.linkedin.com/pulse/netflixs-context-control-how-does-work-steve-urban/ (accessed October 8, 2018).

5. A. Baiyere, J. W. Ross, and I. M. Sebastian, "Designing for Digital: Lessons from Spotify," MIT Sloan Center for Information Systems Research, Research Briefing, Vol. XVII, No. 12, Dec. 2017.

6. Henrik Kniberg, "Spotify Engineering Culture (Part 1)," spotify.com, March 27, 2014. Available at https://labs.spotify.com/2014/03/27/spotify-engineering-culture-part-1/ (accessed October 8, 2018).

7. For an overview of the key concepts associated with microservices architectures and how they differ from monolithic architectures, see M. Fowler, "Microservices," martinfowler.com, posted March 25, 2014. Available at: martinfowler.com/articles/microservices.html (accessed August 22, 2018).

8. Kevin Goldsmith, "Thoughts on Emulating Spotify's Matrix Organization in Other Companies," kevingoldsmith.com, March 14, 2014. Available at: https://blog.kevingoldsmith.com/2014/03/14/thoughts-on-emulating-spotifys-matrix-organization-in-other-companies/comment-page-1/ (accessed October 8, 2018).

9. Ibid.

10. G. Hamel and M. Zanini, "The End of Bureaucracy: How a Chinese Appliance Maker is Reinventing Management for a Digital Age," Harvard Business Review (November-December 2018): 51-59.

11. C. M. Beath, I. Sebastian, and J. W. Ross, "Northwestern Mutual's Digital Transformation: Redesigning IT," MIT Sloan Center for Information Systems Research, Working Paper No. 423, October 2017.

12. M. Mocker and N. O. Fonstad, "How AUDI AG is Driving Toward the Sharing Economy," *MIS Quarterly Executive* 16, no. 4 (2017).

13. Richard Feloni, "LinkedIn Founder Reid Hoffman Shares the Management Epiphany That Took His Company to the Next Level," *Business Insider Deutschland*, March 3, 2016. Available at: https://www.businessinsider.de/reid-hoffman

-explains-why-corporate-culture-needs-to-be-codified-2016-3?r=US&IR=T (accessed October 8, 2018).

14. Sarah K. White, "What is an Agile Coach? A Valuable Role for Organizational Change," CIO.com, August 8, 2018. Available at: https://www.cio.com/article/3294700/project-management/agile-coach-role-defined.html (accessed October 8, 2018).

15. P. Weill and J. W. Ross. *IT Governance: How Top Performers Manage IT Decision Rights for Superior Results* (Harvard Business Press, 2004).

Chapter 6

1. "Predix Platform," ge.com, no date. Available at: https://www.ge.com/digital/iiot-platform (accessed 10/9/2018).

2. D. Cimilluca, D. Mattioli, and T. Gryta, "GE Puts Digital Assets on the Block," wsj.com, July 30, 2018. Available at: https://www.wsj.com/articles/ge-puts-digital-assets-on-the-block-1532972822 (accessed October 9, 2018).

3. For a thorough discussion of ecosystems, see P. Weill and S. Woerner, *What's Your Digital Business Model? Six Questions to Help You Build the Next Generation Enterprise* (Harvard Business Review Press, 2018).

4. 9to5 Staff, "Job's Original Vision for the iPhone: No Third-Party Native Apps," 9to5mac.com, October 21, 2011. Available at: https://9to5mac.com/2011/10/21/jobs-original-vision-for-the-iphone-no-third-party-native-apps/ (accessed October 9, 2018).

5. For more on ecosystems and multisided platforms, see Andrei Hagiu, "Strategic Decisions for Multisided Platforms," *Sloan Management Review* 55, no. 2 (2014): 92–93; and Marshall W. Van Alstyne, G. G. Parker, and S. P. Choudary, "Pipelines, Platforms, and the New Rules of Strategy," *Harvard Business Review* 94, no. 4 (2016): 54–62.

6. "Google Maps Platform," google.com, (no date). Available at: https://cloud.google.com/maps-platform/ (accessed October 9, 2018).

7. "Kabbage Developers," kabbage.com, (no date). Available at: https://developer.kabbage.com/ (accessed October 9, 2018).

8. Google's software development kit (SDK) for their Assistant can be viewed at: "Google Assistant SDK for Devices," google.com, (no date). Available at: https://developers.google.com/assistant/sdk/ (accessed October 9, 2018).

9. M. Mocker, J. W. Ross, and C. M. Beath, "How Companies Use Digital Technologies to Enhance Customer Offerings—Summary of Survey Findings," MIT Sloan Center for Information Systems Research, Working Paper No. 434, February 2019.

10. Ibid.

11. "Our Mission Is to Solve Cash Management for Banks," socash.io, (no date). Available at: https://www.socash.io/about/mission/ (accessed October 9, 2018).

12. "Get a Connected Bank Experience with Your ERP," dbs.com, (no date). Available at: https://www.dbs.com/in/sme/cash/payment/dbs-tally-connected-banking.html (accessed October 9, 2018); in addition, DBS Bank India provides a video that demonstrates how the connection between the Tally ERP and the DBS APIs benefits users: "DBS Bank India, Demo of the Integrated e-Payments Solution by DBS and TALLY," 5/3/2017. Available at: https://www.youtube.com/watch?v=Q6JzkB5SqbA (accessed October 9, 2018).

13. For a current list of available external digital services at DBS, see "Discover APIs," dbs.com, (no date). Available at: https://www.dbs.com/dbsdevelopers/discover/index.html (accessed October 9, 2018).

14. "How It Works," dbs.com, (no date). Available at: https://www.dbs.com/dbsdevelopers/howitworks.html (accessed October 9, 2018).

15. "Meet Uber Engineering's Developer Platform Team, Building Moving Experiences with Uber's API," April 7, 2016. Available at: https://eng.uber.com/developer-platform/ (accessed October 9, 2018).

16. "Riders," "Drivers," and "Uber for Business," uber.com (no date). These three webpages are available (respectively) at: https://developer.uber.com/docs/riders/affiliate-program/introduction; https://developer.uber.com/docs/drivers; and https://developer.uber.com/docs/businesses (accessed 10/9/2018).

17. Megan Rose Dickey, "UberRush Is Shutting Down," techcrunch.com, April 2018. Available at: https://techcrunch.com/2018/03/30/uberrush-is-shutting-down/?guccounter=1 (accessed October 9, 2018); Adam Price, "The Real Reason UberRush Shut Down," medium.com, March 31, 2018. Available at: https://medium.com/@adampricenyc/the-real-reason-uberrush-shut-down-fcb67f166b66 (accessed October 9, 2018).

18. C. Umbach and J. W. Ross, "Your Newest Governance Challenge: Protecting and Exploiting your Digital Services," MIT Sloan Center for Information Systems Research, Research Briefing, Vol. 17, No. 2, February 2017.

19. Philips's ExDP portal is accessible at www.HSDP.io (accessed October 9, 2018).

20. "Schneider Electric Exchange," https://exchange.se.com (no date). Available at: https://exchange.se.com (accessed October 29, 2018).

21. P. Weill and S. Woerner, *What's Your Digital Business Model? Six Questions to Help You Build the Next Generation Enterprise* (Harvard Business Review Press, 2018).

22. M. Mocker, J. W. Ross, and C. M. Beath, "How Companies Use Digital Technologies."

23. Ibid.

Chapter 7

1. M. Mocker, J. W. Ross, and C. M. Beath, "How Companies Use Digital Technologies to Enhance Customer Offerings—Summary of Survey Findings," MIT Sloan Center for Information Systems Research, Working Paper No. 434, February 2019.

2. Ibid.

3. M. Mocker and C. M. Beath, "The First Year of Digital Transformation at Principal International Chile," MIT Sloan Center for Information Systems Research, Working Paper No. 432, December 2018.

4. Our interpretation is based on personal interviews, public information, and two case studies: J. W. Ross, C. M. Beath, and K. Moloney, "Schneider Electric: Connectivity Inspires a Digital Transformation," MIT Sloan Center for Information Systems Research, Working Paper No. 471, May 2017; and S. Scantlebury and J. W. Ross, "Schneider Electric: Redesigning Schneider Electric's Operating Model," MIT Sloan Center for Information Systems Research, Working Paper No. 412, April 2016.

5. Our interpretation is based on two case studies and public information; see M. Mocker and J. W. Ross, "Transforming Royal Philips to Reinvent Healthcare in the Digital Age," MIT Sloan Center for Information Systems Research, Working Paper No. 425, December 2017; and M. Mocker, J. W. Ross, and E. Van Heck, "Transforming Royal Philips: Seeking Local Relevance While Leveraging Global Scale," MIT Sloan Center for Information Systems Research, Case Study, Working Paper No. 394, February 2014.

6. Leah Hunter, "How Philips Digital Accelerator Lab is Hacking Google Glass for Surgeons," *Fast Company*, January 7, 2014. Available at https://www.fastcompany.com/3024202/how-philips-digital-accelerator-lab-is-hacking-google-glass

-for-surgeons (accessed October 9, 2018); and Sean Carney, "What Innovation Means to Me," philips.com, (no date). Available at https://www.philips.com/a-w/about/news/archive/blogs/innovation-matters/what-innovation-means-to-me.html (accessed October 9, 2018).

7. "Philips Opens Its First Co-creation Center to Support Care Organizations with the Transformation to New Models for Connected Health Enabled by Digital Technologies," philips.com, September 10, 2015. Available at: https://www.philips.com/a-w/about/news/archive/standard/news/press/2015/20150910-Philips-opens-its-first-co-creation-center-to-support-care-organizations-with-the-transformation-to-new-models-for-connected-health.html (accessed October 9, 2018).

8. See "Philips Launches AI Platform for Healthcare," philips.com, March 1, 2018. Available at: https://www.philips.com/a-w/about/news/archive/standard/news/press/2018/20180301-philips-launches-ai-platform-for-healthcare.html (accessed October 9, 2018). See also "HealthSuite Insights Overview," philips.com, (no date). Available at: https://www.healthsuiteinsights.philips.com/pages/overview/ (accessed October 9, 2018).

9. Our interpretation is based on personal interviews with DBS leaders, as well as three other sources: S. K. Sia, C. Soh, and P. Weill, "How DBS Bank Pursued a Digital Business Strategy," *MISQ Executive* (June 2016): 105–121; K. Dery, I. Sebastian, and N. van der Meulen, "Building Business Value from the Digital Workplace," MIT Sloan Center for Information Systems Research, Research Briefing, XVI:9, September 2016; and D. Gledhill, "Executing the Digital Strategy, DBS Investor Presentation," dbs.com, November 17, 2017. Available at: https://www.dbs.com/investorday/index.html (accessed October 9, 2018).

Chapter 8

1. "A More Realistic Route to Autonomous Driving," economist.com, August 2, 2018. Available at: https://www.economist.com/business/2018/08/02/a-more-realistic-route-to-autonomous-driving (accessed September 1, 2018).

2. C. M. Beath, M. Tarafdar, and J. W. Ross, "OneBankAssure: Customer Intimacy Through Machine Learning," MIT Sloan Center for Information Systems Research, Working Paper No. 427, March 2018.

3. M. Mocker and J. W. Ross, "Transforming Royal Philips to Reinvent Healthcare in the Digital Age," MIT Sloan Center for Information Systems Research, Working Paper No. 425, December 2017.

4. Cyril Perducat, “Artificial Intelligence: Is the Honeymoon Over?,” blog post, schneider-electric.com, July 16, 2018. Available at: https://blog.schneider-electric.com/building-management/2018/07/16/artificial-intelligence-is-the-honeymoon-over/ (accessed October 9, 2018).

5. Jeff Bezos, “1997 Letter to Shareholders, in 2016 Amazon.com Annual Report,” pp. 5–7. Available at: http://www.annualreports.com/HostedData/AnnualReportArchive/a/NASDAQ_AMZN_2016.pdf (accessed October 9, 2018).

Appendix 1

1. M. Mocker, J. W. Ross, and C. M. Beath, “How Companies Use Digital Technologies to Enhance Customer Offerings—Summary of Survey Findings,” MIT Sloan Center for Information Systems Research, Working Paper No. 434, February 2019.

2. This appendix summarizes content from the book by J. W. Ross, P. Weill, and D. C. Robertson, *Enterprise Architecture as Strategy* (Harvard Business School Press, 2006), especially from chapter 2 “Define Your Operating Model.”

3. J. W. Ross, P. Weill, and D. C. Robertson, *Enterprise Architecture as Strategy*.

4. M. Mocker and J. W. Ross, “ING Direct Spain: Managing Increasing Complexity While Offering Simplicity,” MIT CISR Working Paper No. 390, June 2013.

5. M. Mocker and J. W. Ross, “USAA: Capturing Value from Complexity,” MIT Sloan Center for Information Systems Research, Case Study, Working Paper No. 389, March 2013.

6. M. Mocker, J. W. Ross, and P. Ciano, “DHL Express: Implementing and Maintaining a Global Process Standard,” MIT Sloan Center for Information Systems Research, Case Study, Working Paper No. 393, January 2014.

7. M. Mocker, J. W. Ross, and E. Van Heck, “Transforming Royal Philips: Seeking Local Relevance While Leveraging Global Scale,” MIT Sloan Center for Information Systems Research, Case Study, Working Paper No. 394, February 2014.

Appendix 2

1. M. Mocker, J. W. Ross, and C. M. Beath, “How Companies Use Digital Technologies to Enhance Customer Offerings—Summary of Survey Findings,” MIT Sloan Center for Information Systems Research, Working Paper No. 434, February 2019.

Index